The Metaphysics *of* Love

The METAPHYSICS *of* LOVE

Frederick D. Wilhelmsen

SHEED AND WARD - *New York*

To Virginia

Preface

These studies in the metaphysics of love are offered the reader as meditations written by a man who believes that agape lies at the heart of all being, and who believes that the best approach to agape is by way either of the theology of the Blessed Trinity or the ontology of human existence within history. To those who would follow the higher way, I recommend the works of Richard of Saint Victor. To those whose tastes run to the philosophical, I address this book.

Acknowledgments

The author and publishers wish to thank the following publishers for permission to reprint material used in this book: to Basic Books, Inc., for Rollo May and others, eds., *Existence* (1958); to the University of Chicago Press for Paul Tillich, *Systematic Theology* (1951); to Editora Nacional for Xavier Zubiri, *Naturaleza, Historia, Dios* (1959); and to Yale University Press for Paul Tillich, *The Courage to Be* (1952).

Contents

Contents

Nullius boni sine consortio potest esse fecunda possessio.

RICHARD OF SAINT VICTOR

It is not well for God to be alone.

GILBERT KEITH CHESTERTON

I

Tragedy, Ecstasy, and History

WHEN GOD descended from heaven, man arose from the grave of antiquity and shook off the winding sheet of despair. He walked erect and spoke the name which is His being: Son of God in Christ His Brother. The birth of God was the birth of man, for when God enfleshed Himself in time the human spirit was born. This affirmation does not violate the spirit of philosophical realism. The human person is not simply a being among others thrown into a dumb universe demanding articulation by a voice other than itself. The human person is diaphanous, self-conscious, articulate: this is the structure of its being. Until I know who I am, my person is but the shadow of an actuality and the promise of a future.

That the ancient world had a stunted conception of human personality is a commonplace to modern scholarship. To the Greeks man was at his best when he acted according to a pattern of perfection previously abstracted from the rise and fall of the tides of history. To the Romans man was at his best when he acted out of the fullness of tradition by facing the crisis of decision as did his fathers before him. The philosophical Greeks subordinated man to humanity and the military Romans subordinated him to the City.

The Incarnation of the Son of God gained for us both salvation and personhood. Salvation comes neither to the nature of man nor to the city of man but to men in the dignity of their personhood. The attempt of Arianism to dissolve the divinity of Christ into an ethical absolute marked a last attempt by the classical spirit of humanism to reduce the race of men to the ideal of humanity. The victory over the Hellenizing court by the popular party settled the future commitment of the West to the sacred character of the human person. Roman law and Greek ethics were destined to enter the Christian world, but they were to be given admittance on Christian terms by Christian men, men fully aware that the final law is the law of love and the final City the City of God.

The philosopher who would probe the being of the human person must never forget his history. The destiny of the human person is divinization, union with the Father through Christ. From this point of view, from the angle of finality, we are constituted persons by our beatitude.

I am aware that the above opens me to the charge of "theologizing," of confusing the philosophical and theological orders, of deducing a metaphysical conclusion from a theological premise. The charge would hold were I philosophizing within a rationalist framework in which philosophical progress is conceived to be the manipulation of premises for the sake of the conclusions that can be drawn from them. The charge does not hold if levelled against a man who conceives philosophical progress to be the rendering explicit of what is already given him in being. The being of the human person involves time and is therefore structurally historical. Any attempt to escape this history is bound to issue into a philosophy which will be irrelevant (although not necessarily false) because it will fail to illuminate the being of man as we find him in existence. In the being man has within history, he is destined for union with a Transcendent End. It is *this* human person, the only one who exists, that I am interested in probing in the pages that follow.

But the charge of theologizing is not only irrelevant; it is ironic as well. Issuing from a genuine desire to safeguard the dignity of the natural order and to prevent its absorption into a theological totalitarianism, it fails altogether to realize that the natural order and the scientific disciplines engaged in its penetration came into their own only after the mind of the West had been sealed by the theology of the Incarnation. According to St. Thomas Aquinas, God is not included within the essence of any creature. Were He so included, it would follow that every science would demand metaphysics for its completion. This last is absurd, yet only the West has seen the absurdity. As J. V. Langmead Casserley has insisted, only the Christian distinction between person and nature released the thirst in man to understand the natural world on its own terms. The very concept of *nature*, of an ontological structure functioning within, but in no sense identified with, the metaphysical and the theological permitted that immense growth of natural science within the Western world which is unparalleled in all history. Other peoples have had a genius for science: the Chinese had it two thousand years ago and gave the world the gift of gunpowder. The Arabs had it and filled all the Mediterranean with a nervous mathematics whose supreme achievement is the delicate and distant wonder of the Alhambra. Yet Chinese science dissolved in the mists of moralizing and Arabian mathematics withered in the desert of the Mohammedan religion. Even the Greeks, supreme among the ancients in the appetite for science, mythologized the natural order by absorbing the gods within a cosmos whose final explanation demanded them as immanent principles of unity and intelligibility. The confusion between the metaphysical and the scientific was removed by the Christian distinction between the personal and the natural; this guaranteed science a dignity and promised it a future denied by the non-Christian world.

The Catholic order, in distinguishing person and nature, distinguished questions concerning the *how* of things from the *why*. How I have come into being is an issue belonging to the philosophy of nature and to the natural sciences. Who am I and why is a metaphysical mystery, a mystery asked by men who had been given the answer and hence the question by Revelation itself. Within this tradition, the only one to discover the existence of the person, human *nature* is englobed within the person, is carried by the person, is that ontological structure within which and through which the person acts but which cannot itself be identified with the person. The work of elucidating the meaning of the human person was an enterprise, philosophical and theological in kind, entered into consciously by men who desired to know in a fully articulate fashion the meaning of man so far as that meaning can be illuminated by human reason.

But the mystery of man that the philosopher meditates consciously is the life of man himself in history. The more a man lives this mystery, the more it troubles his heart and stirs his being, the more fully does he become a person. Existential analysis bears out Tertullian's famous *anima naturaliter christiana*. It would be a reduction of Revelation to reason, of faith to ontology, were a man to assert that a phenomenological and existential penetration of the person reveals the Christian dispensation. What must be asserted, however, is that the questions Christians ask in a conscious way, ask because they are Christians, are questions lived by the race of man; even more—this life is the ontological structure of the being of man. Put in another way, we can say that there are questions we ask and questions we are. When I address myself to the nature of the rhombus, the thing questioned is other than myself. When I address myself to the structure of the person, the thing questioned is my being. The answer to this question, the answer to my being, is the Christian God.

Very briefly stated, the question can be formed as follows: What does an existential analysis reveal concerning the ontological structure of man? Setting aside questions concerning the "abstract nature of man," addressing ourselves to men as we encounter them in history, what do we discover? For purposes of organization and brevity I would suggest that we can divide our discoveries into two orders, two dimensions of human existence: the tragic and the ecstatic. Granting that some nations emphasize the tragic and others the ecstatic, granting that these drives are rarely found harmonized within any single man, I think it fair enough to insist that both orders are found within all human beings who have reached the age of responsibility and who act sanely within the world. If existentialist philosophy has proved the tragic, St. John of the Cross and

St. Teresa of Avila, the supreme effort of the Baroque, the whole Counter Reformation spirit, have lived the ecstatic.

What does an existential analysis teach us about the tragic dimension of life? I would suggest that the most cavalier scrutiny of the human condition reveals man as contingent, as finite, as without roots in himself, as lacking the support of the world which is his own, as forever hovering on the brink of nothingness. The death of children, the carrying of coffins, the advent of age, the failure of memory, the cruelty of change, the parting of lovers, the absence of friends, the passing of youth, the knowledge of evil—all these things shake and sunder the being of man. Turn to whomever he might; seek what comfort he can command; marshal what support he can muster, each man knows that in the final reckoning nothing from without can save him from the groundlessness which is his history and his being. Called in a unique manner to care for the things that are, the man who shoulders his task with heroism and realism does so knowing well enough that he is but contingent, that those depending on him depend on a being fragile and without roots.

This is the famous "encounter with nothingness" probed by Heidegger. Nothing is not a thing nor is it a function; it is but a failure in the very heart of our being—a failure promising only the grave. Nor does it suffice, insists existentialist philosophy, to point out the truth that all things die and that death is but the mark of the radical contingency of the universe of creatures. All things die, but only man *has to die*. This *having to die* is not an Aristotelian potency inscribed in the ontological structure of matter; it is an actual menace—better yet, the menace which limits every actual menace—confronting each man who has faced the shock of non-being. In the words of Heidegger, we carry our death before us. In the words of Ortega y Gasset, death is itself the very ground of human creativity. This is not the defiant paradox of a platoon of Death's-Head Hussars or Spanish Legionnaires: *novios de la muerte*—sweethearts of death. Nor is it—far less—the moralizing of a Stoic bore such as Marcus Aurelius. It is rather a truth fingering the being of man himself. Man knows his own contingency. Since man is a knowing-being, the knowledge of his contingency is one with his person. No man is really human who has not faced the meaning of his own death; and only those men who face it daily are fully human. For this reason the Spanish people have always exalted the saint and the soldier as brothers in a common dignity, comrades in a holy company.

Man is the paradox in being. Perpetually falling into the nothing glowering from without and erupting as a hideous void from within, man nonetheless fails to achieve his own failure. He does not cease to be, although everything which is a part of the tragic dimension of existence cries out demanding his annihilation. Nor does it contradict this judgment to point out that men do die in fact, that the only certitude in my future is my own death. Men die, but they never experience their own death. Whatever it be that lies beyond death lies beyond history. Death, therefore, hides itself from philosophical *experience*. The best we can do is to insist that an existential analysis points up the intolerable and yet curiously bracing truth that man is forever threatened by annihilation and yet never is annihilated, is forever menaced by non-being and yet continues to be.

Experiencing the possibility of non-being as the enemy of his being, man senses his finiteness as transcendence. Hunting for an absolute ground to his being, man opens doors and each one of them leads nowhere. Yet he still opens doors. He even does so when he does nothing more than hang on grimly to the shadow of his being, as do those pitiful wrecks of humanity who populate our asylums, driven there by anxiety, haunted by the specter of the face-lessness and silence of non-being. They too continue to be. Each man, therefore, seeks a way out of the insecurity which is one with life. Each man seeks to transcend his own transcendence. Things below man are finite and con-tingent, but only man is driven both to face finiteness and attempt to shake off its sting. Scratching forever in the soil of being, the race is destined to track down a place within which humanity can take root and there flourish within the shadow of the absolute. Transcended by the essence-exist-ence polarity, my being of itself is a transcend*ing* tran-scendence. Man demands a certain and nonfailing ground of being. Humanity makes the demand but not in the sense that the absolute is commanded by the demand: were this so, the facts marshaled above would be phantoms; we would have found a more comfortable world than the one in which we are. Man demands the absolute as the term of his own transcend*ing*—but the Term is not dragooned into obedience by the call of man. The search for beati-tude does not guarantee its fulfillment. In scholastic terms the creature is related to God in its being a creature, but God is not related to the creature in any manner whatso-ever. Man calls for the absolute in the sense that his being is a being-toward Being, a finiteness tending to the infinite in the language of Vico, a thirsting for immortal life in the terms of Unamuno, desirous of God in Aquinas, the soul restless till it rest in Thee in the wisdom of Augustine.

Here the tragic sense of life meets "the erotic" (to use the language of Sombart). The tragic meets the ecstatic. Falling into nothing even while he strives to be, experiencing himself essentially as ontological poverty, man nonetheless must give of himself to the world of things and most especially to the world of persons. The being of man —never sealed hermetically as were the monads of Leibnitz—*is structurally a being with others*. Revealed in the first instance in communication, which is a demand to share meaning with another person; experienced in care, which is the contingent watch over the contingent, the ecstatic drive in man reaches its culmination in love. When a man loves, his being now is a being-for-another. The lover lives literally in the being of the beloved. This is the metaphysics latent in the beautiful phrase, common to many languages, "being in love."

That love is an authentic human experience, that the being of man is achieved only in love, and that therefore the being of man is structurally open to love, are all most forcefully pointed up by an analysis of the negation of love. The negation of love is a self-destroying experience, as are the negations of care and courage. The philosopher does not have to turn to a consciously formulated science of ethics and obligation to validate these ontological ultimates. That they are ultimates can be known experientially: every effort to go against their grain, the grain of being, produces the opposite of the effect desired. Being exacts its revenge when its laws are violated. If love is the free gift of the person to another person, the opposite of love is the attempt to appropriate the being of another to oneself. At the root of every such appropriation there lies the drive in man to conquer his own indigence, to overcome his own ontological poverty. Experiencing himself as limited and finite, the unauthentic human being tries to make up the lack by gathering into his being the being of another. This is quite literally an act of metaphysical violation. If we scrutinize this act carefully, we discover that it involves a vicious contradiction. Hoping to make the being of another a being *for* himself in order that he might fill up what is lacking in his own existence, the unauthentic man ends by turning his own being into a *being-for-the-appropriated*. Thus the miser begins by relating himself to money and ends by being defined by the very money he has appropriated: in a profound sense he has become little more than a being-for-money. Thus the libertine begins by taking into his lust the body of his mistress and ends by being defined in terms of the flesh he has appropriated to himself. He thus becomes the slave of his own conquest.[1] Here is the irony involved in every failure to respect the irreducibility and the dignity of the being of another thing or person: the attempt to make another's being exclusively a being-for-me ends in my making my being a being-for-that-other. This is what I mean by a self-defeating experience. Ontological poverty is not overcome; it is simply accentuated. This poverty, in attempting to feed upon itself, accelerates the deterioration into nothingness it set out to conquer. Thus the demonic thrust for power, be it found in a Faust or a Hitler, is not alone a denial of love in the conventional sense of that word; it is even more a denial of existence itself.

The ecstatic and the tragic meet in a paradox which is one with the being of man. The desire to give and the desire to be fulfilled, the need to throw myself away and the need to be sheltered, are one with human life; logically these drives are opposed; existentially they *are* the being of man. To say all this is but to say that man is not a complete person until he has been loved absolutely, until he has been loved in and by an act of a Person to whom he can give himself freely and who will freely give him—rather *be* for him—the anchor in being that man so desperately needs.

Answered only by the God of Christianity, by the Christ of the Creeds, the being of man—as revealed in experience —*is never revealed as an absolute*. Man's being, seen in the light of both authentic and unauthentic experiences, is a being *for another* and a being *toward another*. "Absolute" means to be absolved from, to stand forth independently from all the rest, to be without being-to or toward. If the preceding analysis is substantially true, we must conclude that man can be called an "absolute" only in an improper sense.

Putting the matter more technically, we can say that there is nothing in man, neither part nor whole, in which he can rest and declare to himself: This is my identity; here I stand secure in the being I am. While forever one in being through an act of existing which confers and in truth *is* his unity, no man can identify himself in the depths of his person with his body or with his soul, with his operations or with his powers, with his origins or with his promise. Even the self-possession of knowledge, the ability of the intelligence to reflect upon itself and possess its own act as well as the thing understood by that act, leaves the soul distinct from its own being. I can speak to myself in the recesses of my being and there discover the I who exists; I can and must affirm explicitly the *I am* who lives implicitly in every judgment. I do gather the whole of my being into a unity of selfhood. But this unity is a metaphysical mystery. Unity, in the metaphysics of Aquinas, comes from the act of existing. Although the ego is one in being, one with itself, it is no more identified with its unity than it is with its being. The self is being and is one through participation in existence. This being that man is through participation is not sealed and closed within itself: it is open—it is destined both to expend itself upon the universe of being and to find therein or in its Source the completion it so desperately needs. It would appear that the human person were better described, not in terms of incommunicability, but in terms of communication and even communion. The person is not circumscribed in being or described adequately in knowledge in terms of the sealed ego. Personality is not constituted by an "I": personality is constituted by a "we."

The attempt of classical idealism and of more than one philosopher within the scholastic tradition to retreat within the self, to seek there deep down within the springs of being some unique principle which is then called "personality"— a principle identified either with the ego or with the ego's consistency and possession of itself—fails to square itself with experience. Some medieval philosophers, well aware that the person was the *totum*, the whole being of man in the full sweep of its history, nonetheless felt constrained to locate human personal*ity*—"subsistence," "suppositality," and so forth—within this or that principle functioning within the totality of human existence. This "something" was looked upon as the center, the zone, the heart from which everything human proceeded and to which everything human was referred. But although medieval Scholasticism did tend at times to "reify" personality, it never made the mistake of identifying the person with "personal*ity*."

This identification was the work of the Renaissance and of the classical idealism which followed. Personality, as Romano Guardini has pointed out in his profound study *The End of the Modern World,* became part of a profane trinity composed of culture, nature, and personality itself. These three summed up being. Beyond them there was nothing. The supreme work of nature, personality harmonized the whole of reality into that City of Man called culture. Personality became the measure of every value and the source of all meaning. In turn, personality and the thinking ego were identified. This self-conscious personality was given somehow whole and entire as a frozen absolute confronting a fluid world which was waiting to be formed by the hand of its master. Classical modernity did believe that personality could be developed and its development was considered the end of culture. But, although capable of development, personality was not altered substantially by this development. The history of a man was personal, but it was not one with his personality, his conscious ego which stood beyond the events as their controlling and appropriating center. Putting the issue in more contemporary terms, we can say that the person acted within history, but he was not a historical being himself.

The *cogito* of Descartes, the Transcendental Ego of Kant, and the concretized Spirit of Hegel could well be studied from this point of view. Suffice it to say that all of these philosophical fictions were elaborated out of a single climate of intellectual opinion. Man was looked upon as the sole subject of existence and he was this sole subject not in his total historicity, but only in that self-conscious principle, the ego, which confronted a world of objects with which it was associated in varying degrees of intimacy and distance. The philosopher today who approaches the mystery of the person comes to it weighted by this philosophical background. He tends almost mechanically to seek some ultimately self-identified principle standing behind or within the concretely existing human person. Rejecting, often with scorn, that popular wisdom which identifies "personality" with the sum total comprising any given human being, the philosopher usually seeks his explanation in a principle given at the outset of human existence, a principle accounting for the uniqueness and incommunicability of the human subject before him. Briefly, the abstract term "personality" is thought to refer to some real ontological factor within the total concrete complexity of the human person. This factor, once again, is usually associated or identified with the thinking ego. No matter how often the charge of "staticism" is denied, the suspicion remains that the human person somehow lies behind all it does, sole responsible agent for its activities, possessor of all its qualities—but not *really* either those of action or character.

The argument at this point once again demands a recourse

to history. The ingrained prejudice of the philosophical mind of modernity in favor of locating personality in the self-possession of an ego can be traced to the myths we have inherited from the Renaissance, myths conditioning our conscious philosophical meditations because they are the stuff from which we disengage meaning. The entire subject-object opposition, unknown to the thirteenth century, illustrates and clinches the point at hand. St. Thomas Aquinas, St. Albert the Great, and St. Bonaventure lived in a world in which the *subject* was the ultimate in being, that existent fingered in all judgments as reality itself, ultimate "subject" of affirmation and denial. The *object* was the subject as known. The Renaissance and the philosophies issuing from its spirit destroyed this old world. The sole subject of being became the thinking ego; the "object" became the content of the thinking subject. The subject was thus identified with the thinking ego. This isolation of man from the totality of being entailed divorcing him from history, from a world of subjects in which he—admittedly the most exalted—played out his role. To phrase it very briefly, we might say that medieval man understood the subject of being to be the thing he knew, whereas modern man understood the subject of being to be the one who knows. The consequences for any understanding of the historic human person are immense.

This shift in emphasis and doctrine was occasioned by a shift in culture. Unless the latter be seen clearly, the metaphysical issues cannot be understood. The history of culture does not enter philosophy simply as a rhetorical device for the illustration of doctrine. History is part of philosophy not only in the sense that philosophical doctrines have consequences which come to roost fully only in the course of time. History *is* philosophy in that history is the soil from which philosophical intelligibility is disengaged. The intelligence of man—the *active* intelligence, the *lumen* through which man participates in the Mind of God— draws all its meaning from an imagination and sensibility forged in the fires of historical existence. The conventional picture of the serene philosopher meditating the meaning of a distant cosmos which impresses itself upon his spirit as a seal upon wax is a myth. The philosopher is not the nude thinker of classical sculpture: he is a clothed and broken cripple, as are all human beings. He brings to his task a body and a mind, an imagination and an emotional commitment, a heart. All philosophers bear the scars of history. To say this is not to write an apologia for the weaknesses of philosophers: it is to point out something integral to philosophical existence, something proper and necessary to the life of wisdom. The scars of history, after all, are often badges of honor. We are historical beings and we must philosophize within history. The only distinction at this level is between those men who philosophize within history and know it and those who philosophize within history and do not know it. It is the latter who are the dupes of history. My position is by no means the same as that of those men who maintain that we must know our history, our cultural antecedents, in order to purge them carefully from our minds before we begin to philosophize. This is rationalism covering its tracks. A philosopher of existence must never shake off his history. His history—as Eric Voegelin has so magisterially demonstrated in *Israel and Revelation* —is that form of being which came into being as a result of man's experience of his own participation in existence. The philosopher, therefore, must come to know his history so that he might use it intelligently and delicately, often reverently, in his search for the meaning of being.

In the light of the above remarks and in the context of this meditation, let us pose the following questions in all their historical generality: From what cultural sources, from what imaginative springs, from what symbolic framework did medieval philosophy draw its data in its attempt to elucidate the structure of the human person? By contrast, from what cultural structures did the classical ages of modernity draw *their* data? The answers to the questions will not determine the truth about the human person, but they will determine the relevance of the respective answers given. It can never be emphasized too often—it is emphasized altogether too rarely in American philosophical circles—that truth is not the end of philosophizing. The end of philosophizing is *truth which is relevant to the human situation*. Should we discover that the ages of modernity philosophized about the person out of a context irrelevant to the human situation, then we need not bother ourselves with an elaborate and detailed study of the internal inadequacies of the systems in question.[2]

Now I contend, as indicated, that medieval man meditated within a world of existent subjects. His culture was pre-eminently a spoken culture, a *personal* culture. Things were written down in books for the sake of memory, for the sake of the spoken word. Living within a historical world, full of the give-and-take of dispute, medieval man philosophized—quite literally—with things and men before his eyes. Classical idealism was born into a world in which that old medieval community of learning had already been broken to pieces. Idealism drew its intelligibility, abstracted its meaning, neither from men nor from things. Meaning for classical modernity came from the written word. The Protestant emphasis on the written word as the source of all truth; the solitary conditions under which Descartes, Spinoza, and even Leibniz did their work; the rapid spread of the printed page—all tended to make philosophers see the ultimate data of their discipline as things having their actual existence upon the written sheet of paper before the eyes. Sense images drawn from a "book culture" (to use a term made popular by Herbert Marshall McLuhan and Walter J. Ong, S.J.) are spatial. They lack change, as does space itself. The only way things can change in space is by changing place. The only progress in a purely spatial universe consists in rearranging static elements already given within a frame resembling a picture frame hanging on a wall. (Does not the diplomatic history of the eighteenth century look like a pleasant game of musical chairs to us today?)

Sense images drawn from this spatial civilization were in turn frozen into abstractions made to function as ontological absolutes. Thus the grammatical subject, written on a piece of paper, stands anterior to, and spatially separate from, its predicates, its "objects." This grammatical subject worked its way into the psyche of modern philosophy; it became the sole subject of existence, the self-contained "ego" thinking a world beyond itself, "outside itself" just as the written "ego" is spatially "outside" its determinations. In this way the concrete person was hypostatized into an absolute, into an abstract personality to which the whole of reality referred itself for validation and rationality.

Ortega y Gasset has pointed out that the Middle Ages are actually more distant from the psyche of contemporary man than are the ages of classical antiquity. The modern world, product of both the French Revolution and the earlier Renaissance, has sought its origins in the ancient world and thus has attempted to leap over the Middle Ages as though they had never existed.[3] It requires, therefore, an unusual effort of the imagination today if we would capture again the spirit of the high Middle Ages. I would suggest here that this effort can be made easier for us if we bear in mind the simple fact that medieval man *never* sensed himself as an absolute subject, as a distant personality viewing existence as a field to be exploited or as a theater to be enjoyed. The life of men in those centuries was the life of the soldier; his destiny was the defense of Europe against the infidel from without. The bastion of the Faith, Europe was a living shield behind which Christendom built itself up, layer upon layer, until the spirit of the Gothic burst the heavens and lanced the Godhead in the springtime of its youth. The superb youth of the Crusades, laughing—in the deathless prose of Hilaire Belloc—"under its pointed cap of steel and resting upon a two-handed sword, the irony and the strength, the grotesque of the cathedrals, the virile energy of the Faith, the reach of all those endless high arches, the strange indefinite hopes that led upward and outward ceasing"—all figured themselves upon the sinew of the medieval heart and lent a magic dignity to the swords and lances of the knights of Christendom. Defend the

town from the enemy beyond the walls; within, prepare
for the leap to God. The walls and spires of Europe, the
castles of Spain: these make a better testament to the spirit
of Catholic Christendom than all the unread and forgotten
commentaries on the logic of the ancients. An intellectual
age, it was nonetheless a time suffused with the thrill of
danger and the risk of defeat. In those days the *Te Deum*
was the hymn of marching soldiers and the hair shirt was
often worn under chain mail. Knights Templars, before
their decline and suppression, slept in open graves the better
to prepare themselves for the nervous scimitars and delicate
mounts of Islam. The ashes of Lent, the corpus on the
crucifix; the *memento mori*—all made life the good fight
of St. Paul. Medieval man believed in but one Absolute,
one Lord. Human dignity was something achieved, won,
fought for under the banner of the Cross. A civilization of
soldiers and monks and peasants is never tempted to confer
upon itself the attributes of Divinity.

But the Middle Ages lost their nerve by the first quarter
of the fourteenth century, and a kind of corporate anxiety,[4]
itself reflecting an entire civilization's encounter with meaninglessness and nothingness and dread, fell upon the West
and demanded expulsion in the very name of sanity itself.
The anxiety was dissolved in two directions: in the Reformation, which accepted sin as the very condition for human
existence; and in the Renaissance, which lifted man out of
his tragic destiny by investing him with a borrowed divinity
that covered over the skepticism with which he could not
cope, and which was itself but a manifestation of late medieval anxiety.

It was upon this exhaustion that the Renaissance broke

like a welcome sun from the south. It came upon our civilization as a fresh and healing breeze, promising relief from anxiety and release from the burden of contingency. It came proclaiming the absoluteness of human personality. Never denying the one God, forever affirming that man truly is one in dignity only under God, the Renaissance was nonetheless a reaction to pagan antiquity. This reaction is but imperfectly understood today. The Renaissance was an assertion of the independence of man, of his absoluteness. Renaissance man was the lord of a serene and lovely world, an earth yielding its fruits graciously and easily to its master. This master exercised his dominion over the things that are as a natural right, a right resting on the excellence and beauty that were one with human nature. Renaissance man was a revivified Platonist. His beauty was that of classical art; his matter, the perfectly formed human body, nude, purged of all eccentricity and individuality, formed after the pattern of a Greek athlete; his language was that of line, not color; his art form was sculpture, not portraiture. Without inner contradictions, he took as his model in morals the *Nichomachean Ethics*. An aesthetic rationalist, Renaissance man made all things conform to the ordered and decorous pattern of an intelligence purged of all save its own perfections. Viewing himself in the mirror of the world, calmly, with neither passion nor prejudice, objectively as befitted a man formed in the image of Greek moderation, Renaissance man looked upon himself and found nothing wanting.

The Renaissance, for all its majesty—or possibly because of it—was in a sense a denial of the human situation, of the tragic and contingent mystery of man's existence in time and history. Its spirit found its most perfect contradiction in Cervantes, whose Don Quixote and Sancho Panza symbolize the tension that lies at the heart of human existence. This Hispanic reaction to the paganism of the Renaissance is perhaps best summed up visually by the Escorial and the painting of Velasquez: the one, a brooding monastery-palace—massive, granite, squared all round and topped by a cupola, reposing under heaven as a sign of man's utter dependence upon God; the other, the soul of Spain etched in the somber magnificence and the irony of that Velasquez who painted kings and fools and peasants, but who painted the Greek gods of antiquity only to mock them. His drunken Apollos and Venuses, painted from peasant models, affirm with sardonic humor a people that refused the peace and humanism offered them by the classical spirit of the Renaissance.

Without in any sense pining romantically for a culture stripped of its dependence upon the Renaissance inheritance, permit me nonetheless to insist that its conception of human personality was blind to the paradox of ecstasy and tragedy that our phenomenological analysis of human existence has disengaged as central to the meaning of man. Anxiety is not exercised by exalting man into a quasi absolute, and the Council of Trent laid it down as a first principle that only the grace of God can heal despair. Despite the Renaissance glorification of all things human, man continued to experience himself, as indicated, as a dynamic whole in being, paradoxically falling and failing to fall into nothing, called to give his being to the world of persons and other beings. Experiencing himself as structurally open to the whole of reality, man in no sense is a sealed monad closed within the lonely splendor of his own subjectivity.

The human person, demanding fulfillment and demand-ing to fulfill, is the face of Janus in being. Looking back to his origins, he is simultaneously propelled forward to the fullness of his perfection. The German language, in the very word *Person*, has preserved an awareness of the per-son as something settled in being at the outset of his exist-ence, given in his origins as a reality destined perhaps for fulfillment but standing now at the commencement of his history as an ultimate. *Ein Person steht davor.* Thus might a servant announce the presence of one beyond the door to his master: who the stranger is and why he stands there are unknown both to servant and master; yet it remains eternally true that a person asks to be admitted. Guardini, in the work cited already,[5] has pointed out that the person in this context is an ontological ultimate. Undeveloped, without nourishment, altogether lacking in human interest, the naked person is created by God as an ultimate in being. Tell the mother dedicated to a child sick in body or mind that only the "full development of personality" confers perfection upon a human being and she will fly at your throat! The person is sacred simply in being, and quite often the very absence of "personality" is precisely that which brings home tragically and absolutely and beauti-fully the sacredness of a human thing. Every Christian must salute this starved and stunted reality as the image of Divinity.

Guardini's contention that in a mass age the person must resign himself to forgoing the development of his "per-sonality" is both true and false, or so it seems to me. It is true in that "the well-rounded man" is *not* he for whom

Christ died, nor is this lingering Renaissance myth man as
he was created by God the Father. Guardini is wrong,
however, in that the person—existing as he does in time—
demands fulfillment in history. Where such demand is impossible the tragic dimension of life is the further accentuated, as it is in our age. But life is tragic enough as it is
without worsening the situation in the name of commitment to mass society! The progressive fulfillment of the
person is what popular speech refers to as "personality."
By contrast to the German, the Spanish language has preserved an awareness of the identification of the person with
his history. Not only has Spanish tended to suppress the
personal pronoun and thus merge the agent acting, the
"subject," with the verb—the action exercised—but the
Spanish language, because of its poverty of nouns, has
tended to designate with adjectives, to name the person by
his qualities. The fact that you are this or that is subordinated to whom you have become through the course of
time: thus women will be named by their age and men by
the way they *appear* to the senses, that is, as "the tall one"
or "the ugly one." The famous Suarezian denial of any
distinction between essence and existence might well be, as
Pedro Lain Entralgo has suggested, a remote philosophical
reflection of this Spanish propensity to identify a being
with its concrete appearance, its manifestation and presen-
tation to the world, its "unconcealedness," in the language
of Heidegger. Without pressing the point, we can certainly say that the Spanish language itself suggests a psychology that sees the human person as identified with what
he does, with his acts and his qualities.

The Austrian novelist Musil, in writing a book called

The Man Without Qualities, described a metaphysical monster. Man as we find him is not only implicated in his qualities; he *is* his qualities in all the existential profundity implied in the verb "to be." Here the experience of love is crucial. The attempt to love a person for his or her qualities—be they spiritual or physical, intellectual or temperamental—deteriorates into a kind of prostitution in which the person is used and valued for what he does and has. Relationships based on the mutual admiration of qualities end in disillusion and often in bitterness. Built on the lie that the person is exhausted in his qualities and actions, the "love" in question crashes inexorably on the rock of reality. Conversely, the attempt to love a person in abstraction from his qualities,[6] be they good or evil or indifferent, results in a cerebral and bloodless relationship which at best is an illusion and at worst a denial of the historical person himself. Richard Weaver has pointed out that great personalities are often loved precisely because of their failings, these last being somehow bound up with their very genius.

These truths lead me once again to a single conclusion. The human person is that whole in being who, experiencing himself as finite and contingent, without any grip on his own being, nonetheless exists within an order of being to which his own being is open and in which he must seek his destiny, even to the surmounting of the world and to the giving of himself to a Being who, in no sense needing him, nonetheless gives Himself and thus heals the wounds of contingency.

If these considerations are to be understood in depth, they require a careful probing of the meaning of being. In this context the danger of a latent rationalism points in two directions, that is, in making the "openness" of being follow upon being or of making being consist in its very "openness."

The statement that my being is "open" could mean that my being is *also* open. First, I exist through an act by which I am being; second, this act of being relates itself to the universe of being. Implicit in this reasoning is the conviction that the act of existing has a certain "formal" effect: the placing of a being outside its causes. Such a universe (there is evidence that such was the universe of Cajetan) reduces the act of being to the empirical factuality of a fully constituted substance.[7] Within such a world the existence of any given thing, once *there,* is also able to be related to the whole of being. But this "also" is a post-Greek residue weighing down a Christian metaphysics struggling to come into its own. What could "also" mean within the order of being *as being?* It could only mean "nothing" because an "also" to being is an above and beyond being. But above and beyond being there is nothing at all.

Hidden deep within this conception of being is the Aristotelian distinction between substance and accident. When this perfectly valid *essential* distinction is carried over into the order of existence, the act of existing becomes *substantially* that by which I am, *accidentally* that by which I am related to others; this latter, in turn, is looked upon as the "openness" of being.

The distinction between substance and accident permits us, of course, to think within the essential order wherein the distinction makes sense. It is without any value when applied to the order of existence: what a thing is "substantially" and what it is "accidentally" do not alter the truth that the thing *is* in both these ways. Essential distinctions cannot be located within being *as being*. To conceive the act of existing as that by which I am primarily and that by which I am related secondarily is to make existence actually being and potentially relation. Not only does this destroy the cardinal truth of St. Thomas' metaphysics that *esse* is in every sense act and in no sense potency, but it also clouds the community that being *is*. Every being is an "opening," an "appearing," a presence, a call. Briefly, in being I am a being-to or toward other beings. This "being-toward" does not follow upon my being: it is one with my being.

The danger to this position is that it might fall into an identification of being with "openness," into a metaphysics that sees being defined by its very relatedness to other beings. In such a philosophy *to be* would mean *to be toward*. *Esse* would mean *esse ad*. Prompted by a valiant effort to shake the staticism haunting so many ontologies, this metaphysics is prey to the error it would exorcise. To make the being of a creature exclusively a "being-for" is to reduce the meaning of being to the category of relation. Being is thus described in terms of its direction, in the prospect of its future, in the light of the things to which it is related. The universe of being is thus frozen into a mosaic of relations in which nothing truly is, but in which all these nothings are related one to another. Against the intention of the men advancing such propositions, the irreducible dignity and character of being is weakened. More deeply, being itself is described structurally in terms of its otherness, its incompletion. To describe being as otherness, to see being constituted *as being* in the light of its direction, to understand being as a "for-ing" rather than as an "is-*ing*" is to introduce non-being into the structure of existence. Paul Tillich, for instance, does not hesitate to do this, nor did Plato before him. It is doubtful, however, whether such a position can be maintained by a Thomism fully conscious of its own inheritance. Altogether apart from these systematic considerations, let us address ourselves to the following question, the crucial question in this context: What is it that is manifested in being? What is it that erupts into the whole theater of existence? What is it that appears open to the whole and as related to the whole? Is it "manifestation" that is made manifest, eruption that erupts, openness that is open, relation that is related? Only a man devoid of the sense of being and of the meaning of language itself would presume to answer in the affirmative.

Therefore, I sum up my position in the following paradox: being is not constituted by its openness; being is constituted being by simply being, but every being is open *of itself*.

This metaphysics of being permits us to confront the concrete historical person on his own terms. Among other considerations, it permits us to understand how and why a man can sense a distance between the whole that he is and his ego. Experiencing myself as a whole, knowing that I am my most distant modifications and every act that I do, I nonetheless experience a tension, a duality, between the ego who is the whole being and the whole being that the ego is. I am able to experience a distance between all I am and that center of my being which can call itself the ego. It was this distance that lent a certain plausibility to the wall classical idealism erected between personality and

the world, between subjectivity and objectivity. It was
this distance that sent latter-day scholastic epistemologists
scurrying for proofs that man had an arm or a leg or a
hand. After all, only the most extroverted and empty of
men have not felt a fissure between the inner ego and the
whole person. Hemingway's Santiago in *The Old Man and
the Sea*, having fought the shark for days, finds that his
left hand is failing him. Borne down by the unequal struggle, near death from fatigue, the old man speaks to his left
hand, rebukes it for not being what a left hand ought to be,
calls upon it to do its duty in the fight still to come. Thus
it is that we can often objectify this or that member and
scrutinize it from a distance. This experience is most common when we are sick. We sense our being as dissolving
about us; we retreat into the depths of subjectivity and
there watch—sometimes with morbid interest, more often
with a kind of desperate helplessness—the progressive deterioration of the being we are. Thus the body of a sick man
often seems to him to be little more than part of an external
world floating before the eyes of his spirit. There are
analogous experiences within the moral order. What man
has not halted in mid-career and looked with horror at the
paltriness of his life, at the foundations half-built, the fail-
ures in love, the ashes of expectation? These experiences
reveal a fissure between the ego and the whole human
person.

When the experience is controlled for the sake of philosophical penetration, we find ourselves (if I may use a
spatial metaphor for a nonspatial reality) in a retreat into
the distant recesses of our being. We tend to rest finally
within the soul, not as within a principle concluded to

"from without," but as to a reality grasped "from within." We conclude, often enough, that the self thus discovered is the soul. We may even be tempted to imagine that here we have found an absolute ground of personhood and being. The danger in all this is the temptation to reduce the body to an instrument, perhaps an instrument of a special kind, but an instrument nonetheless. The philosopher who takes this road ends finally in affirming that he *is* his ego (that is, his intellectual soul) and that he *has* his body.

The metaphysics involved in this reasoning is lacking in delicacy and is insufficiently controlled by a sophisticated phenomenology. These experiences point to man's contingency, to the tragic dimension of life probed earlier in this chapter. But none of these experiences reveals an absolute identity of the ego with its being; none of them permits me to affirm that "I am my soul and I have my body"; rather, they point to the contrary. The ego who exists is a unity in simply being the ego it is. Not only does the intellectual soul need the body in order to be the intellectual soul that it is, not only *am I an ego only through being a body*,[8] but I am not the existence through which I am and am one. End situations—particularly those involving anguish and the confrontation with nothing, the awareness of impending and inevitable death, the menace of evil, the weakness of the spirit—are situations in which the ego, gathered now into the center of its spirituality, fully reflected upon itself, open to its being, experiences that very being—its very own—as sliding away from itself.[9] Here is the final cross upon which the human spirit must hang. Here is the last road and one of its forks is marked with the sign of despair.

The recovery from such experiences is the recovery of the unity in being, just as the recovery from physical sickness is a taking of the body once again into the whole man who is. Ontologically, these crises contrasted with their normal counterparts point up the paradox which is man. Experiences of limitation and alienation form the tragedy of life; experiences of fullness, the wholeness and goodness and decency of life. The first look to the multiplicity in which I am created;[10] the second look to the existential unity of that very creation.

Although one in being, although existing by an act through which substance and accidents, soul and body, "powers" and operations are one, this being is in no sense identified with any of its parts taken separately or with all of them taken together. I can experience the being of my body as distant from the being of my soul because my unitary act of existing—common to soul and body—belongs immediately to my soul and through my soul to my body. The body participates in the being of the soul: this accounts for the sense of distance. But in St. Thomas, unlike in Plato, to participate is to be the participated because the participated is the act of *is*. Put in another way, we can say that the state in which essence (of itself non-being and hence nothing "by nature") is placed by *esse* is *ens*: I really *am being*, but this being is not mine by "nature"; it is mine by participation. This accounts for the awareness of being one, of unity—unity being nothing more than the undividedness of a being from its existence. This permits me to affirm that "I *am* my body, my operations, my powers." *Esse* is the most intimate of all principles, insisted Aquinas. Most distant from matter because matter is alto-

gether passive and receptive, *esse* is closer to form, the
vehicle by which the body exists; in no sense identified
with any form, *esse* is uniquely associated with *that* spiritual
principle which is the human soul. Here the composite
exists through the very being of its formal component, so
that existentially man is entirely spiritual, even though essentially he is both spirit and matter. Yet even here *esse* is
other than the soul.

The human person is the whole being. His personal*ity*,
ultimately, is communion with God in love. The historic
denial of this truth evidences again the revenge of being
upon its enemies. The search for personal perfection, for
personality, through an identification of the person with
the "sovereign" ego, produces the anonymous *Geist* of the
Hegelian idealist tradition. The search for personality
through an identification of the person with the body (as
in contemporary mechanized culture and as in any form
of materialist civilization) instances the savage reprisal
existence visits upon those who tamper with its laws. The
narrowing of the person to the body involves an objectification of the body. Every objectification of a part of man
entails a retreat of that part from the whole man. I need
"distance" in order to scrutinize anything "objectively." I
need to get outside the reality in question in order to see it
calmly "as it is." This is perhaps necessary, for instance,
to the athlete who trains and conditions his body for the
contest before him. Not only is that athlete one in being
with his body along with the rest of the race, but that body
has become an object—a thing—subjected to a highly cere-
bralized discipline imposed upon it by the will. There is no
danger in such an objectification, provided it be kept

within strictly defined and highly artificial limits, anymore than there is a danger in ascetical exercises when kept within limits for the sake of the end in question. Should these limits become blurred, the structure of being finds itself under attack. Thus the frightening objectification of the sexual in our industrialized Western culture has produced the opposite of what was intended. Hoping to find peace and union in sexual expression, man has turned the sexual into a thing which stands outside his interior subjectivity. He has turned the sexual into an object manipulated mechanically for the sake of biological reactions which are only hideous puppets of the reality they mimic. Instead of becoming the sexual, man has transformed it into an exterior thing waiting on exploitation and degradation. The final result is that modern industrialized civilization is the most sexless in all history.

A man for whom his body is an object is a man without a body. He is not a man at all. The same depersonalization can be traced in the drive for power, in which men are often tempted to seek their perfection. As long as power is linked with the body in a reasonable proportion, as long as I can sense or at least imagine the things over which I have power, I can act as a responsible agent, as a person fully accountable for my acts. But the divorce of power from personal responsibility, the divorce of power from the *human body*, progressively corrodes the sense of responsibility itself. Thus an airplane pilot, to use an example given by Bernanos, who would hesitate to crush out the life of a butterfly, will trigger without the least hesitation the bomb that sends thousands to their death. No longer experiencing any personal responsibility for the power he exercises;

aware of power only as an abstract object grasped through the manipulation of a handful of gadgets—man soon becomes a prey to his own servant. Cut away from the person, power thus tends to objectify itself and to master its servant. The end is still further dehumanization, the price we must be willing to pay for our refusal to understand the unity and integrity of the human person.

There are those who would avoid the mystery of human existence, or at least soften its tragedy, by returning to some form of humanism. By humanism I mean in this context that doctrine or program that would relate the whole order of values—be they spiritual or material, artistic or religious—to man considered as a kind of absolute ego capable of appropriating to himself the whole of existence. The humanist attempts to get outside of history in order that he might relate the whole of being to man. Aware of the dignity of the human person, he would arrange the cosmos hierarchically and then fit it to the structure of humanity. He would cut the cloth of reality to fit man. His intention is admirable and wherever it functions we can be certain that some measure of respect for humanity has found an incarnation. But the humanist program lacks reality because it fails to see that man, as he exists historically, never stands beyond the cosmos of things and values; man is never in a *position* to actualize the humanist dream. Man as he is is always implicated in the cosmos of things and values and therefore finds himself as a being *related to* rather than as a being who *relates*. As I am, I am thrown into a world to which I am willy-nilly related and within which I must carve out whatever destiny Providence has decreed as my own. A humanism might possibly be preached to an academic community privileged to live in isolation from the broad sweep of history. Humanism can never be preached to a peasant or to a soldier or to a beggar or to a king. Caught within a world to which they are structurally and ontologically open and to which they are related by their very stance within existence, such men—and they are merely convenient symbols for all men because this is the situation in which each one of us finds himself—cannot abstract themselves from this their history in order to find peace and excellence within an abstract order of humanist values; they must find their destiny within their situation, within their concrete historical roles. Often this destiny demands the death of the humanistic ideal: what night watchman supporting an aged mother, a sick wife, and a handful of children can make his own the humanist program of education, aesthetic sensibility, intellectuality, that light— *Licht*—the the great Goethe called for upon his deathbed? The salvation of such a man—and he is no abstraction; all of us are so implicated and thus limited by history in varying degrees of tragedy and glory—is found in direct proportion to his ability to give himself to the world, even should this giving require the suicide of his finest sensibilities and the withering away of his every possibility for humanist excellence and fulfillment.

Hoping to save man from the iron grip of history, humanism would withdraw man from the tragedy of existence and therefore from the call to ecstasy. The humanistic search after security can take a literary form and then it calls for a return to the golden age of classical scholarship and art. The search can become Jungian psychology and then it calls for a retreat within to the timeless and mythic springs of the psyche. The search can become philosophy and then it urges upon us, as do Robert Hutchins and Mortimer Adler, "The Great Conversation" over the ages and a liberal education for the masses; it proposes a dialogue between men who seek virtue and wisdom in ideas and goals cut away from the soil and the burden of history. The search can become the dream of a "New Christendom," the integral humanism of Jacques Maritain, a dream that frankly confesses itself tired of history and its tragedies.[11]

Implicit in every humanism is the conviction that man—somewhere, somehow—contains within himself (even if only under God) the source and ground of his own perfection. Provided only that we can cut this source away from the impurities of history, provided only that we can locate the center of the person in some absolute ground transcending the world, then we can rescue this isolated personality from the ravages of time and contingency. The failure of humanism cuts two ways:

First, humanism identifies the person with sealed incommunicability and then identifies this sealed ego with the soul. The identification is weighted heavily with the ghostly inheritance from which it came. If the ego is considered to be the intellectual soul itself, then the ego is *not* the person anymore than the ego is the whole man: the person and the whole man are one. If the ego is considered the whole being as self-conscious of its activity *through* the intellectual soul, then the ego is truly the person. It is that person who says to himself: "I am this man, flesh and blood, bone and spirit," a man related in a uniquely historical manner to the whole of reality, a man situated in a world proper to himself within which he must carve out salvation and personhood.

Second, humanism, in hunting *within* a sealed person for his person*ality*, neglects the openness of being which is the very finality of man. Destined for fulfillment, called to beatitude by a God who created him in order that he might love and thus fulfill another, be loved and thus be fulfilled, the human person becomes himself through time and history. Not only subsisting in his existence, he tends by that very existence—St. Thomas teaches in the *De Veritate*—toward an end in which he can rest, fully perfected and finally at home in the being who he is. A full personality only when united in love to God, man's being—because it is open—is structurally relational. Since every relation involves both that which is related and that to which it is related, the personality of man in its total existentiality is not an "I": it is a "we." But this "we" is the term and the transcendence of history. And history is harsh because the way of history is the Way of Sorrow. Seeking within for something to underwrite the coin of being, Renaissance man thought he had found the treasury in the supposed self-sufficiency of human subjectivity. Latter-day existentialism has proved the coin counterfeit and the treasury bankrupt. But the poverty of man is his glory. We Christians have known this because we are the people of God.

Notes

1. It should be clear from the text that we have passed beyond the conventional tension between "objectivity" and "subjectivity" in order to reach structures within being itself. Therefore, it is irrele-

vant whether the libertine, for example, is "subjectively" satisfied with his conquest. Ontologically, *he* is the one who has been conquered. Should he fail to see this, his *real* situation is all the more pitiable because he has achieved a modicum of happiness only by drawing a veil between himself and existence. He has become a sleepwalker.

2. The reader ought to be warned that the text makes certain concessions to current prejudices. Had I been writing strictly within an epistemological framework, I should have had to say that irrelevant truth is simply not truth at all. Here pragmatism, Thomism, and existentialism meet in an astonishing concord that has yet to be explored in depth and detail. The pragmatic (Jamesian) contention that truth is verification of meaning in the real, the Thomistic contention that truth is an existential relation between meaning and being, and the existentialist contention that the "truth" about which I do not care is not truth at all are three distinct insights bearing on the same "truth," a truth about Truth. Unless I am related to the real in the knowledge situation, I cannot *care* about that situation; and unless I am able to find (that is, to *verify*) some being in which this "knowledge situation," this meaning, has existence, I cannot know whether it is true or false. Any abstract meaning or "intelligibility" that is not related to existence lacks precisely that bent toward being which constitutes truth as such and which gives birth to care. Newman felicitously distinguished between an assent which was "notional" and an assent which was "real." The schoolboy hearing lines from Horace for the first time assents "notionally" to their truth. It is only after much living in the world that he *really* assents to the wisdom of what he read as a child. Yet it seems to me that Newman was being too kind to rationalism. An "assent" which is not real is not an assent at all, or at best it is an assent to Authority but not to *what* Authority has proposed as the truth.

The relevance and *therefore the truth* of meaning demand a world of beings to which meaning is related. This world of being, for those of us blessed with the privilege of living within Western Christian civilization, is largely—although not exclusively—historical. (I say "not exclusively" historical because it is always possible to confront a raw and untamed nature, a nature untouched by the hand of man.) It follows that philosophical truth is inseparably linked to history. It follows that metaphysics cut away from history is irrelevant and therefore, while not necessarily false, certainly not true. Such a "philosophy" may have pedagogical value; it may train the mind; it may give the student an illusion of reality not easily supplied by exercises in formal logic. It may be quite useful in its way, but it has nothing to do with philosophy.

3. José Ortega y Gasset, *Castilla y sus Castillos* (Madrid: Afrodisio Aguardo, S.A., 1956), pp. 95–101.

4. Cf. Paul Tillich, *The Courage to Be* (New Haven: Yale University Press, 1954), pp. 57–63, for an account of "periods of anxiety." It is only fair to add, however, that my own interpretation of medieval anxiety differs somewhat from that of Professor Tillich. My interpretation owes much to Hilaire Belloc's *Paris* (London: Methuen, 1923), and to Thomas Mann's *Doctor Faustus* (New York: Alfred A. Knopf, 1948).

5. Romano Guardini, *The End of the Modern World* (New York: Sheed & Ward, 1956).

6. The reader will note that I wrote "in abstraction from," not "in spite of."

7. Etienne Gilson, "Cajetan et l'existence," *Tijdschrift voor Philosophie*, Vol. 15 (1953), pp. 267–286.

8. Cf. Anton C. Pegis, "St. Thomas and the Unity of Man," in James A. McWilliams, S.J., ed., *Progress in Philosophy* (Milwaukee: Bruce Publishing Co., 1955), pp. 153–176.

9. Cf. the classical statement: Martin Heidegger, *Was ist Metaphysik?* (Frankfurt: Vittorio Klostermann, 1955).

10. We reach here an ontological mystery whose only "explanation" is the unintelligibility of sin. *A priori* there is no reason why multiplicity should breed tragedy. *De facto* this is so. Christians know that the integrity of the human substance was shaken by original sin, thus introducing a fissure into the harmony that ought to have reigned within the person. For this reason contingency is a *threat* to human existence. The living within this threat is what Paul Tillich calls "the courage to be."

11. Cf. Jacques Maritain, *Reflections on America* (New York: Charles Scribner's Sons, 1958), esp. pp. 25–29, which are significantly entitled "Deliverance from History."

II

Being as Ecstasy in Contemporary Spanish Philosophy

José Ortega y Gasset

IF A PHENOMENOLOGY of human existence points to the person as a structural cross between ecstasy and tragedy, this phenomenology must nonetheless remain radically insufficient unless it be penetrated by a metaphysics of being, a metaphysics which is both prompted by and which illuminates the analysis in question. Putting the matter in other words, we can say that a truth about human existence points beyond itself to a truth about existence as such, a truth which in turn can bend back and illuminate its point of departure—human existence. Our point of departure in the first chapter of this study was the tragic and ecstatic within the life of the human person as we encounter him within history. Setting aside for the present the tragic and concentrating upon the ecstatic, I will address the reader's attention to whatever it might be that ecstasy reveals about the very meaning of being as such. Although we could reach far back into the springs of the Western tradition, to St. Augustine for example, to the Franciscan spirit, or to

Richard of Saint Victor, let us limit our analysis here to what two contemporary Spanish philosophers have to tell us about the meaning of ecstasy. Their conclusions, I believe, ought to illuminate what has gone before as well as teach us truths which are consubstantial with the very meaning of being.

I have not chosen two *Spanish* philosophers capriciously. The Spanish national temper suggests that union of personality and history within an ecstasy of being that our phenomenology has uncovered. The finest Spanish philosophical speculation in our time has been called forth by the Spanish preoccupation with the meaning of historical existence. There can be no doubt that this ferment is due to Spain's concern about her own future and therefore with the meaning of her own past within the economy of Western Christendom.[1] But although often prompted by immediately political ends, this passion for the historically concrete is deeply rooted within Spain's philosophical inheritance. A penchant for human values marks the Spanish temper and anneals the nation into the thing it is. The emphasis on the human and on subjective density goes hand in hand with an indifference toward the cosmic, the natural. According to the eminent psychiatrist Juan Lopez Ibor, "the Spaniard reacts instinctively to human, not cosmic, values. His aggressive instincts are not directed against or toward the physical world as are those of Faustian man, but toward or against other men."[2] In Greek tragedy, for example, human destiny is wrapped within the mystery of the order of the world. Man works out his salvation within a natural scheme of things of which he is a part and to whose order he must attune himself.[3] The same simply cannot be said of Spain. Don Quixote wanders through a world of inns, windmills, palaces, robbers skulking at the side of the road, men on horseback seen from a distance. Like the monotonous La Mancha whence came the Sorrowful Knight, nature exists but to reveal a tower, a sentinel, a voice in the night, a human thing. In Spain and possibly only in Spain man is what Dilthey thought him to be: more history than nature.

The historicity of man was captured brilliantly by the same Lopez Ibor in an essay dedicated to the problem of "sincerity."[4] Sincerity, a virtue highly valued in the Anglo-Saxon world, receives a searching scrutiny from the jaundiced eye of the Spanish psychiatrist, who believes that the virtue—as commonly understood or misunderstood—lacks realism and therefore genuine candor. The public confessions of a Rousseau or a Gide, aspiring to the purest sincerity, fail precisely because they run counter to the historical structure of human existence. Man is never frozen in such a moment that he can say to himself: this I am and neither more nor less. No man ever really is simply what he imagines himself to be at any one moment, solidified and thus removed from the moving stream of time. The very projectory character of human existence involves a tension between actuality and expectation. It follows that we both are and are not what we would be. We are what we would be because we are defined by the tendential structure of our being: the arrow in a sense is already the target. But being an arrow, the arrow is not its destiny or its end, its target. It follows that the historical dimension of the being of man demands a conception of being that is open, ecstatic.

Spanish metaphysical speculation today is marked by a reluctance to admit any "static" or "naturalistic" theory of being because such a theory does not do justice to the open and historical structure of human existence. As a result, contemporary Spanish philosophy tends to consider the problem of being and the problem of history as aspects of the same ontological mystery. The meaning of being must *integrally* implicate the meaning of man. This way of coming to grips with the ontological unites thinkers who are separated in everything else, and it even cuts through the profound political and religious divisions that have sundered the Spanish mind in two since the French invasion of the early nineteenth century. A preoccupation with the being of history and with what might be called "the history of being" unites liberals such as the late Ortega y Gasset with Carlists such as Rafael Gambra[5] and Juanists such as Rafael Calvo.[6] It even unites them all with the supremely apolitical and even Olympian figure of Xavier Zubiri, widely considered the finest metaphysician in Spain.

The present chapter is limited to a consideration of two men who have devoted more than an incidental portion of their philosophical careers to the problem of being as related to the meaning of history: José Ortega y Gasset and Xavier Zubiri. Both conceive of being as open and ecstatic. Both have been influenced by modern German philosophy. Both see Aristotle as the discoverer of a dynamic notion of being, but both believe he failed to exploit his own discovery. The two thinkers differ in that they understand the above issues in their own ways. They also differ in that Ortega was not a Catholic throughout his intellectual career, regardless of what his intentions may have been shortly before his death, whereas Zubiri—a Catholic—has a doctor's degree in sacred theology and has been profoundly influencd not only by medieval Scholasticism but even more by the Greek Fathers of the Church and by the thought of St. Paul. Finally, both of them say things that might well be meditated by those contemporary Thomists who see in St. Thomas' metaphysics a unique existential approach to being.

So far as Ortega is concerned, let us limit our discussion to one crucial work by "the philosopher of Madrid," his *Ideas for a History of Philosophy*, which was published in a larger volume under the title of *History as a System*.[7] Throughout the entire study Ortega confesses his debt to Dilthey, whom he considered the greatest philosophical figure of the nineteenth century because of his revindication of theoretical dimension of history and because of his refusal to reduce man to a fixed and stable nature.[8] This latter doctrine Ortega roots in the Greek world, especially in the Eleatic and Platonic mind:

In few philosophical themes can we see with such clarity the extent to which European man is the heir to the Greek mind. But an inheritance is not only a treasure; it is also a burden and a chain. Masked under the concept of nature, we have received the chain which has made us slaves to the destiny of Hellas.[9]

Ortega considers the concept of nature to be inexorably linked to what he calls "the Eleatic concept of being," being as fixed and static within the *state* that it *already* is. Pre-Aristotelian philosophy, viewing mathematical objects and visual objects as the prototypes of being, looked upon change as a kind of degradation, as a ceasing-to-be-what-you-already-are. Ortega sees the naturalism of Boyle and the tradition of Comte and John Stuart Mill as moving in an erratic line from the Eleatics through Aristotle down to modern times.[10] This tradition, convinced that the ultimate in reality is invariable law and self-identity, is the born enemy not only of the humanistic tradition of the West but of the philosophical attempt to justify that tradition in a radically ontological manner through the revival of the concept of history. History cannot be reduced to nature, but history is the ontological dimension proper to man. The insights of historicism, often proceeding from men who had abandoned Revelation, nevertheless came forth from minds annealed in the conviction that the Western Christian experience could not be understood philosophically by a tradition rooted in the pagan mind, a mind whose fundamental philosophical discovery was *physis*, the structure of the physical but not of the human universe. As Zubiri, at one time a student of Ortega, has put it, the supreme tragedy for the Greek mind is age and decay, whereas the supreme tragedy for the Christian mind is nothingness.[11] The former grew out of what Zubiri calls the "horizon" within which the Greek mind operated, the horizon of fixed natures whose dialectical enemy must be the ceasing-to-be-of-*what*-once-was. The Christian experience is one with the "horizon" of a created and contingent world whose opposite is the nothingness out of which God called it into being. If historical existence cannot truly be absorbed into the *nature* of the classical world, it does not thereby follow that it cannot be absorbed within the contingent and existential world of Christianity.

In the light of these questions it is more than instructive

to follow Ortega as he tries to shake man loose from the Eleatic concept of being in order to redeem his historicity. In the work in question his tactics display themselves at their best in two distinct cavalry charges made against Eleaticism, the first a meditation upon the meaning of "having been" and the second an anlaysis of the antinomies within the Aristotelian teaching on being.[12]

In his first meditation Ortega advances the thesis that man cannot *be* what he has *been*. "European man," he writes, "has been a 'democrat,' an 'absolutist,' he has been 'feudal,' but he is these things no longer." Quickly clarifying himself, Ortega distinguishes by insisting that man *is* these things, is his past, but only in a certain manner. Man continues to be his past but "in the form of having been it."[13] Once having been his past experiences, once having passed through them and finished with them, man can no longer be them. The future is determined by the past precisely because the past determines what the future *cannot be*. "Having been something" automatically impedes my being that thing once again. In a daring reversal of the usual formula, Ortega affirms that the irreversibility of historical time is rooted in the irreversibility of man's historical action and not the other way around. "Time never turns back upon itself because man cannot turn back and be what he has already been."[14] It might be objected against Ortega that factually a man *can* reverse himself: for example, he can fall back in love with a woman with whom he has fallen out of love; he can reverse his political convictions and return to those he inherited from his father; he can return to a life of scholarship after having left it for a time. Although Ortega does not meet this objection to the best of my knowledge and although his choice of examples often lays him open to the same question, I believe a close reading of the Ortegian text can answer the objections on Ortega's own grounds. In the instances cited, the "having been" is chronological, not metaphysical. The man who recovers political convictions held in his youth never underwent the *full* experience of having lived through the convictions in question. His new adherence is born of a new understanding into what he once held. He now becomes a believer in democracy or in monarchy, let us say, with a new insight into what was once seen but imperfectly, and therefore not really lived through intellectually in an authentic sense of the term. But should a man have truly experienced either political philosophy in the depths of its profundity and should he have lived through that experience authentically in the sense of having rejected it or in the sense of having carried it into a higher synthesis, it would be ontologically impossible to turn back. To turn back would involve the past's contradicting itself. It would involve my not having seen what I once saw, not having adhered fully to what I once believed, not having been what I once was. The past, insists Ortega,

is past not because it has been passed on to others but because it forms part of our present. It is that which we are in the form of having been it; in short, *our* own past. Life as reality is absolute presence: one cannot say that something is *given* which is not present, actual. If the past be given, it shall have been given as present and as now acting within us.[15]

Ortega concludes by saying that if we insist upon applying the Eleatic conception of being to man; if being be retained in what he calls its traditional sense of "being-already" (*ser ya*); if being is what is fixed, static, invariable and given, then it follows that the only being we can discover in man is what he has been. "The past is the moment of identity in man, whatever there be of *thing* within him, the inexorable and the fatal."[16] If man has no more Eleatic being in him than his having-been, then it follows that his authentic being—what he really is as standing in the present moment of time—consists precisely and formally in "being what he has not been," in a being which is non-Eleatic."[17] Despairing of liberating the term "being" from its static and traditional sense, Ortega proposes that we disengage the genuine meaning of what men have been accustomed to call "being" from the term itself. Here is the very nerve of the philosophy of vital reason (*Yo soy yo y mi circunstancia*), whether it be found in Ortega himself or in his prolific contemporary disciple, Julian Marias: at all costs we must erect a concept larger than being in order to account for the dynamism and openness of man's historicity. Man, continues Ortega, is not but rather "comes be-ing" (literally, *va siendo*) this or that. Nevertheless, the notion of being as a "comes be-ing" is ridiculous on Eleatic grounds which sees being as the fixed and completed. But were we to convert the historical "comes be-ing" into the concept of life, we would have transcended the Greek category and, having done so, would have affirmed that man *lives* rather than is. When I give an account of any physical-mathematical reality, I give that account in terms of a nature expressed in a law. When I give an account of anything human, I do so by telling a story.[18] Ortega appeals here, not to the abstract nature of man attributed by him to the tradition, but to a concrete, lived accounting of any given man as we find him in existence. Man *is* what his pilgrimage *has been*, but man's *life* is greater than his being because man's life looks out to what he has not been but to what he can be in the light of what he once was. The only nature of man is the fixed trail he has blazed, or, to alter the figure, the wake he leaves in the sea of time. Although concerned with giving a justification for a history which would simultaneously be a system—because it would be rooted in an exact knowledge of what man has been, itself fixed in the timelessness of the Eleatic precisely because it is the past itself—Ortega is concerned primarily with justifying the supremacy he had given life over being, at least so far as the ontological situation of man is concerned. The systematizing of the *cognitio rerum gestarum* is founded in man whose vital reason produces an essence out of *rerum gestarum* that are the work of his own hand and spirit. "The past," he adds as a corollary, "is not out there in its own year but here within me. I am the past."[19] But my life is bigger than my past and therefore broader than my being.

But when the Philosopher of Madrid returns to the same issue later on in the work in question, he seems disposed to find a concept of being that would fit the life of man. He does this in the concluding sections of his *Historia como Sistema* in a remarkable exegesis of a number of crucial Aristotelian texts on change, on act and potency, and on immanent activity.[20] Taking as his point of departure Aristotle's celebrated assertion that thought is a "progress" toward itself," Ortega advances the thesis that Aristotle wavered between two conceptions of being—the Eleatic or "static" and the dynamic which was his own discovery, a discovery marking an enormous progress over Plato and the entire Greek tradition prior to Aristotle himself. Ortega sees Aristotle as the discoverer of the active meaning of being, but he sees him as a man who was frightened by his own discovery. The philosophy of Aristotle, writes Ortega, is one long attempt at solving the problem of movement, a problem whose solution eluded prior Greek speculation because of its propensity to see in being a supreme and undisturbed rest, a self-identity, an absolute metaphysical repose. Ortega calls this the "spectacle" theory of being, being as it actually appears to the human eye, where things rear up and confront the field of vision as figured and colored objects, completely and totally one with themselves. This is being as scenario but not as drama. In an even more typically Ortegian phrase taken from his own pages, this is a world of "things as paralytic as are purely geometrical bodies."[21]

But Aristotle's awareness of the real prevented his reducing change to an epiphenomenon. Change is a passing from being one determined thing to being another determined thing. A white thing and a black thing are fixed and determined, structured, quiet, at rest. But the passing from one state to another, from white to black, is neither a being-white nor a being-black. This is "being on the march" from whiteness to blackness. Ortega's analysis at this point follows the traditional analysis of the Aristotelian teaching. If the thing which is actually white were in no sense black, it could not become black. It would have to be annihilated and its place taken by a totally new reality. There would have been no change. But if we conceive the thing which is actually white as being potentially black, we have found a key to the problem of change. This does not involve white's being actually black; it simply involves white's containing the potentiality or the power to be black, a power which is latent within white and which commences to act as a power only when white begins to become black. The reality of change, therefore, is "a strange mode of being which reunites the two opposed characteristics of potency and effectuality."[22] Potency is an imperfect act, a reality which is beginning to be fully act but which has not terminated in being so.

Aristotle's "it is truly difficult to understand what is change" is the fatigued groan of a man wiping the sweat from his forehead, says Ortega.[23] It is the tiredness of a man who has remained faithful to the real despite the pressures of a philosophical inheritance that had hitherto refused any effective actuality to change whatsoever. "The business is difficult to see, but we have to accept it as it is."[24]

Although content with this ontology of change, Aristotle's subtlety forces him to probe the issue further because reality presents him with two kinds of "change" which *terminate* in two distinct ways. In one kind of change, the change which motivated the above analysis, there is a distinction between the change itself and its term. To become black is not the same thing as being-black. But there is another kind of "movement," best exemplified by the life of man: the movement involved in thinking, loving, meditating. The transition from not-thinking, not-loving, not-meditating to their acts is a "liberation of the potency as such."[25] But the transition from not-thinking to thinking is "to-be-now-thinking." There is no distinction between the term of the act of thinking and the act of thinking itself. Ortega gives precision to his understanding of Aristotle on immanence by pointing out that the act of building a house results in a house built, something standing in existence independently of the act of building it. This is a work concluded, finished, an instance of the static being of the Eleatic tradition.

But let us imagine that the work we aspire to do consists precisely in a doing, in an action, as when we propose to ourselves that we take a walk without having in mind any place to go. In thought, therefore, as in every change, there is a transition and a passing, but paradoxically enough thinking is not a passing to *another* thing. On the contrary, it is an enlargement, a course, an advance or a "progress toward oneself."[26]

Ortega notes that Aristotle restricts the term "change," *sensu stricto*, to the first kind of transition and reserves the term "act"—*energeia*—for those "changes" which do not progress toward anything else but whose end is immanent to themselves. Ortega concludes here that Aristotle has transcended the static concept of being because he locates this act, this *energeia*, at the very heart of being itself. "The effort needed by a Greek to conceive of being as pure mobility is extreme and it is interesting to note that Aristotle, in arriving at this height of his own thought, arrives exhausted, panting for breath, and from then on he wavers."[27] Even in defining movement or change-to-the-other in the strict sense, we have seen that Aristotle raised his hands to his head as though dizzied by vertigo. At this even higher point we find Aristotle utterly unable to push on and draw from his own discovery their more profound metaphysical conclusions.

Thus far we have seen Ortega the exegete, but now we confront Ortega the philosopher. Had Aristotle insisted more upon the opposition between change in its strict sense and the "change" typified by the act of thinking, he would have said that, whereas movement is the act of a being in as much as it is in potency, the *energeia* typified by thinking is the act of a being "converting itself into its own potency, *actuality as potency*."[28] If the dynamism of immanence gave Aristotle vertigo, we can say that the Ortegian actuality which creates its own potency must do the same to anyone trained in the scholastic tradition! Yet Ortega's explanation of his own obiter dicta, while paradoxical, does not land him in any obvious contradiction. The act of thinking or of loving is nothing other than a constant renovation of itself. Once I have thought A, I am able both to continue thinking A and to think A again in a series of acts which renew the first act of thinking A. "In this series the 'second' act reactualizes the first which has converted itself into the potency of the second and so on."[29] Ortega shrewdly adds that what surprised Aristotle was the fact that the passing from the initial potency to think into the act of thinking does not imply "the destruction of the potency but rather the conservation within the perfection of the entelechy in such a manner that potency and act assimilate one another."[30] The potency which is actualized is born again as a potency which subsequently reiterates its own actualization. Once I have become grayhaired, I cannot become gray-haired again; but once I have meditated on God, I can meditate on Him again. The first case involves the destruction of the potency and the second its renovation through the potency's very actualization.[31] "Therefore the kind of movement which reiterates its own actualization—act, *energeia*—is not finished when it reaches its term because its term *ad quem* is the same as its term *a quo*."[32] In reaching its perfection the act has bent back upon itself and reclaimed its own potency. This is Aristotle's progress toward itself of the *De Anima*.[33]

Aristotle, maintains Ortega, in this the supreme glory of his philosophy, saw being from within itself and thus transcended the static conception of being endemic to the Greek world. A reality such as the act of thinking or loving is a *doing* which engenders its own perfection from within itself;[34] it is an act which is its own potency.[35] The Aristotle of the entelechy is the Greek who returns to the visual and spectacle concept of Plato and the Eleatics: that is, of a being which rests in its end as in something finished, whole and complete within itself. This is being as seen by the naked eye, being as understood—let us say—by a boatbuilder who, having put the finishing touches on a dinghy, stands back and contemplates with satisfaction this work of his own hands as something achieved and done. Ortega would add something "done with" because the deeper and dynamic conception of the real is found in the Aristotle of the *energeia*, who sees being from within as active and as exercised. With satisfaction the Spanish Liberal maintains that *this* Aristotle is supremely modern, an Aristotle who would have relished Goethe's "in the beginning was the Act" and Fichte's "being is pure activity."[36] When people talk of Aristotle's "dynamism," they ought to take seriously the words they use, insists Ortega. The key to this dynamism is not actuality but the very *dynamis*, the potentiality, itself the creation of actuality.

Ortega's reading of Aristotle on being agrees perfectly with his own emphasis on the historicity of human existence. If being is the finished and over with, being as nature, as "has-been," then being is a *definition* of my nature. But if being is dynamic potentiality and self-realization, then it structures the historical dimension as such. History is both tradition and future because being is both a "progress toward the self" and an engendering of the self. That Ortega ultimately preferred to call this fullness of past with present and future "vital reason" may be due to the idealist shading of his own epistemology. In any event, Ortega sees being, at its deepest level, as one with an immanent activity which both recapitulates the past within the present and which, because of its structurally "unfinished" character, does justice to the ontology of history.

Xavier Zubiri

BEFORE CONSIDERING Ortega's understanding of the dynamic structure of being in the light of St. Thomas' metaphysics of existence, let us turn to the thought of Xavier Zubiri.[37] Zubiri recognizes a positive and a negative aspect to historicism. Human existence is something which *happens*. It is history. But beneath the happening which is history there is something which endures: man as nature.

Man as both nature and as history must be bathed in a metaphysics of being that does justice to both of them. "Today it is necessary that we introduce the very concept of history as such into the very idea of being as Aristotle introduced movement and change into that same notion. . . . But as Aristotle transcended the pure mobilism of the Sophists, so too must the ontological interpretation of history avoid a radical historicism."[38] Zubiri's attempt to grapple with the problem of history is the very best introduction, I believe, to his metaphysics of being as ecstasy. Zubiri distinguishes carefully between the *powers* of man and his *possibilities*. The former belong to his nature but the latter to his history. The exercise of the natural powers of man demands a field of possibilities which are not themselves given with those very powers. A man with nothing other than powers, nothing other than nature, could not act because he would lack a "field" within which he could exercise his humanity. Such a man would be a man without a history. History is the field of possibility for the powers of human nature. From the viewpoint of possibility itself must be understood the articulation of past, present, and future. The past does not live on as a reality which underlies the present. History, therefore, ought not to be considered as though it were a snowball which grows in size as it rolls down a snow-covered hill. As a reality, the past is simply dead and gone forever:

But the past is not reduced to nothing. The past derealizes itself and the sediment is the possibility which it confers upon us. To pass does not mean to cease to be, but to cease to be reality in order that the possibilities it yields man might define the reality of the present situation. In the sixteenth century feudalism had died, but European man had become something else, thanks to the possibilities open to him as a result of his having lived a feudal life. What we are today in our present is the convergence of the possibilities we possess as a result of having been what we were yesterday. The past lives on under the form of possibility.[39]

The doctrine is summed up trenchantly by Zubiri in one sentence: "History is neither a simple 'making or doing' (*hacer*) nor is it merely a 'to-be-there-being-able-to-do' (*estar pudiendo*); history, rigorously speaking, is the 'making of a power' (*hacer un poder*)," the power for the future created by the possibility of the past.

There is a relation between Zubiri's understanding of history and Ortega's and both probably owe something to Heidegger. Both Ortega and Zubiri see history, "the has been," as possibility, but they differ in that Ortega views this possibility as negative and defining whereas Zubiri sees it as a positive field for the future. Both Ortega and Zubiri are conversant with Heidegger; however, I would suggest that there are significant differences between Heidegger and the two Spaniards on this issue. For Heidegger, I organize my past in the light of the intentional structure of my *Dasein*.[40] The past, while a field of possibilities, is a field of *meaningful* possibilities because of the ecstatic structure of existence.[41] The differences between the three men might be expressed as follows. Ortega: the past is a meaningful structure defining the future negatively. Zubiri: the past is a meaningful structure defining the future either negatively or positively, depending on human freedom. Heidegger: the past is a meaningful structure whose meaning derives from the future, from the ex-statis of *Dasein*.[42]

It is clear that Zubiri, as well as Ortega, is unhappy with the concept of being as he has inherited it from the scholastic tradition. For Zubiri the past is not a reality; nonetheless it is not reduced to nothing. If one equates being with reality as frozen to the present moment (that is, Ortega's Eleatic being), then possibility is neither being nor is it reality, but nonetheless it is not nothing. The plurality of meanings given the verb "to be" is patent, and it is adverted to more than once by Zubiri, who was among the very first European thinkers to point up the ambiguity in the Aristotelian teaching on being. In 1935 Zubiri maintained that "philosophy, for Aristotle, is not a science of being (that is, 'as such') because Aristotle never arrived at any *one* concept of being.[43] If the first meaning of "being" is taken from the "is" which affirms the reality of subsisting things, this meaning—teaches Zubiri—must be corrected when the verb "to be" is applied to the intelligence. Man's "being" is a "being-open-to-things," which is first revealed in the "is" of the act of understanding which consists in being an "is-other." Simultaneously, this "being-other" is a return of the intelligence upon itself: the more I go out to the other, the more I become the self I am. This very return of the intellect upon itself as well as its openness to the real reveals the inadequacy of the concept of being taken from subsisting material reality when applied to the being of man. As a result, maintains Zubiri, the ontological dialectic is not the simple application of a ready-made concept to a field of diverse objects, nor is it only an amplification of that concept made under the pressure of that

diversity. The dialectic of being is a progressive "constitution" (intentionally) of the very field of being itself. The
discovery of a second order of being forces me to return
to my point of departure and deepen ("radicalize" is his
favorite verb) my original understanding of the ontological structure of the real. Referring to the medieval
doctrine of the analogy of being, Zubiri suggests that we
distinguish between a concept and a *ratio entis*.[44] The concept of being is an intellectual formalization of an insight
into some meaning consubstantial with being itself. There
are not only many concepts of being, but there are many
rationes entis. The ontological dialectic is principally the
discovery of these *rationes*. Moving from the being of
things through the being of man to the being of God, the
metaphysician finally reaches the meaning of Being Himself. Each advance within this dialectic involves—if I may
repeat myself—a return to the older *ratio* and its succes-
sive "radicalization" in the light of the newer. The end of
metaphysics would be the bathing of all being in a *ratio
entis* which was born itself of an analogical understanding
of the *ratio divinitatis*.[45]

Zubiri develops and uses this framework both in his
study on the meaning of history and in his essay "The
Problem of God," but the doctrine comes to fruition in
his remarkable work on St. Paul and Pauline teaching in
the light of the theology of the Greek Fathers of the
Church.[46] What the Spanish philosopher actually did was
write a metaphysics of love. Zubiri begins by laying down
as a general historical truth the proposition that the Latin
Christian mind has tended to see love primarily as an act
of the will, as the perfection of a faculty, whereas the

Greek Christian mind has tended to see love primarily as constituting reality in its most profound center. For the Latins love is principally moral; for the Greeks it is principally ontological. The latter see the dramatic unity of human existence as a tension between agape and *eros*. Both can be called love because both are an ecstasy, an ex-stasis, a "standing outside of oneself." They are differentiated in that *eros* is a standing outside of oneself for the sake of one's own perfection: I seek the other in order that I might find myself. *Eros* is the ecstasy proper to nature because all finite beings seek the perfection engraved in their natures. Agape is personal love in the sense that the lover seeks nothing *for* himself, but rather affirms the richness of his existence in conferring it freely upon the other. But this free gift, although formalized in the will, is one with the structure of personality. Zubiri appeals here both to Richard of Saint Victor and to Alexander of Hales as Latins who held this typically Greek doctrine. Its specific meaning will emerge later on within this essay.

The New Testament assertion, repeatedly made by both St. Paul and St. John, that God is agape was taken by the Greek Fathers in a strictly metaphysical sense. Our Western tendency to read the Greek Fathers in a metaphorical and devotional sense has drained their thought of real interest and meaning for us. In order to understand the patristic agape we must return to *their* understanding of the classical Greek metaphysical vocabulary. Appealing again to his contention that there is no *one* meaning of being within Greek metaphysics, Zubiri turns to the very same antinomy that Ortega discovered within the mind of Aristotle. The dynamic notion of being will supply the

Greek Fathers with a metaphysics for the scriptural *agape*. Aristotle, in moving toward a unified understanding of reality, had before him two models upon which he could construct an ontology: the example of material being and the example of living being. Zubiri adds that, although these two were nothing other than examples, in time "they took their revenge, the one upon the other."[47]

The mode of being of purely material beings was a "being-there" (*estar*). Stability or immovability marked the plenary character of being taken in this sense. Change or movement always indicated imperfection, an imperfection from which the material thing emerges or an imperfection into which the thing is submerged. But the mode of being proper to living things inspired another conception of being:

In living things, movement is not merely mutation; whatever there be of mutation in the living thing is nothing other than the external expansion of a more intimate movement which consists in life itself. To live is not simply "a being-there" nor is it simply a changing. Life is a kind of movement more subtle and more profound. . . . The peculiar character of living being as movement and not as mutation was designated by the term "immanent." Stability—*manere*—is not a simple absence of vital movement but the full expression of an internal living movement; reciprocally, whatever there be in life in movement is not only not primarily a mutation, but it is the very realization itself of the *manere;* this is what the prefix "im" means in "immanent." If we lay aside whatever there be of mutation in vital movement and concern ourselves with the simple internal *operation* of to live, we shall understand what Aristotle himself means when he tells us that the being of living things is their "to live" understood as an immanent operation. . . . Aristotle thus calls being *energeia*, the substantial operation in which being itself consists. In this sense of the term, being is the more perfect the more mobile, the more operative it is.[48]

At this point Zubiri points to the equivocation surrounding the Aristotelian *energeia*, which the Latins translated as "act." In the first sense of the term "being" as applied to purely material things, act means *actuality*, that which effectively *is there* being. But in the second sense of the term, the term as applied to living things, act means *activity*, that which effectively is *be-ing*. Quoting Dionysius the Aeropagite, Zubiri asserts that being as living is ec-static: the more being there is, the more that being diffuses itself dynamically. Employing a metaphor drawn from the text of St. Bonaventure, Zubiri states that being in the static or material sense can be likened to the quantity of water contained in a tank; being in an active sense can be likened to the spilling over of running water which simultaneously both fills and overflows the tank. In the first sense, being is a term, the actualization of a potency; in the second sense, being is a principle, activity itself. Through its living acts, the living being "comes to be" that which it already was (*el que ya era*). Summing up the differences between these two conceptions of being so far as they apply to the finite order, Zubiri maintains that being is always *received* in the static and *executed* in the dynamic sense; being is "there" as something fixed and complete in the static conception, and being is a primitive and radical action in the dynamic conception.[49]

The classical philosophical term *dynamis* was taken by

the Greek Fathers in two ways, maintains the Spanish philosopher. It could mean a potency which emerged from the *ousia* which demanded it for the fullness of its unity and perfection, or *dynamis* could mean the expansive perfection of life itself, the fullness of power, vitality, strength, the ex-stasis of being. In the first meaning of the term, *dynamis* indicates something defective or at least finite in being; in the second meaning, *dynamis* looks to fullness and perfection. The Greek Fathers so stressed this second meaning that they considered the activities of living beings to be principally the unfolding of the original richness of *ousia*.[50] The more finite is a being, the more powers (in the scholastic sense of the word) it needs in order to come to grips with the world and thus achieve its own perfection, being, *eros;* the more being approaches the unity of the Divine, the more its activities are absorbed into its *ousia* as into a sheer dynamism, an activity whose purity consists in being its own act, or—in the words of Zubiri himself—"in subsisting as pure action, as pure *energeia*."[51] Our author finds in the Greek Christian tradition an ontological unity between *agathon*, *bonum*, and causality. The tendency of each finite being to seek its own good is one with the erotic structure of existence. In going out to my end, I return to my self and in exercising my own being, I go out to my end. Essence for the Greeks is not what it was for the Latins—the ontological correlative of a definition. Essence so understood is the finished, something that has been. (The parallel with Ortega is obvious, but it is doubtful that Ortega knew he was repeating a patristic saw!) For the Greeks, essence is the radical activity constituting being as the very root of all its manifesta-

tions. Essence is something active, a "to-essence" manifested in the *dynamis* which are the *truths* of *ousia* because they are that which make *ousia* known.[52]

Up to this point Zubiri writes in such a manner that he
justifies the contention made by many Europeans that he
is the living Catholic philosopher most capable of entering
into a dialectic with Heidegger. The Heideggerian analysis of language as a key to being; the Heideggerian doctrine on Truth as the unconcealment of the concealed; the
Heideggerian teaching that the truth of being is a "letting-
being-be" which in turn is "being's-coming-into-the-
work" (*ins Werk setzen*); the Heideggerian identification
of glory with being's revelation of itself through its un-
concealed state—all are themselves Greek themes which
Zubiri has made his own. But whereas Heidegger sees the
Greek mind as falling into decadence with the advent of
Plato, Zubiri sees the genius of the Greek spirit—sown as
seeds in a pagan world—come to its fruition in the mind
of patristic theology.

When the Greek Fathers turned to God, they meditated
upon a Being whose Infinite Activity (Zubiri does not
hesitate to say that for the Fathers God is pure *Action*) is
so absolutely One with Himself that His diffusiveness is
totally gratuitous. Needing nothing, God's word spoken
into nothingness which makes things be is pure love,
agape. Hitherto agape and *eros* were mingled, but now
the full meaning of agape as the *ratio* of all the *rationes
entis*, the meaning of the meanings of being, emerges. In
God the ecstatic character of existence in no sense grows
out of a poverty but is one with the richness of Divinity.

Zubiri approaches the issue by effecting a synthesis of

the Greek patristic mind on the meaning of personality. Being a synthesis, the doctrine is stamped with the originality of its author.[53] Appealing especially to Richard of Saint Victor, himself inspired in a very special way by St. Basil the Great, Zubiri chooses to denominate personality a "relation of origin":

The whole of my nature and my individual perfections are not only *in me* but they are *mine*. There is in me, therefore, a special relation between what I am and the one I am, between the *what* and the *who*, between nature and person. The nature is always something had; the person is he who has. But this relation can be understood from two points of view and the sense of "having" is radically distinct in both perspectives. One can see in the person the pre-eminent way of realizing the nature, the ultimate term which completes the individual substance; but one can also see in the nature the manner in which I realize myself as a person. Thus the person is not the complement of nature but a principle for its subsistence. . . . I am myself and my individual humanity, I am that which has come to me and in which I consist in order that I might be able to subsist. For the Greeks, person is formally constituted by a relation of origin; that which constitutes nature is, in a certain sense, an abstract and brutally given datum, as individualized as one cares to view it. Richard of St. Victor introduced a terminology which fared badly in history but which is frankly magnificent in itself. He called the nature a *sistentia* and the person the manner of holding the nature, its origin, the "*ex.*" As a result, he created the word *existentia* to designate the unified structure of personal being. . . . The person *sistit* but as coming "from" someone. This "*ex*" expresses the supreme grade of the unity of being. . . . In order that one be a person, his personal being must

be referred to someone from whom he has received his nature
and also to someone who can share that nature. . . . Thus we see
how the *eros* of the nature takes on a new character. The effu-
sion and expansion of personal being is not the natural tension
of *eros:* the person expands and diffuses itself through the personal perfection which it already has. This is donation, the
agape which leads us to God and to all mankind.[54]

Person, designated as it is by a personal *name* which has
been given me, is (let us gloss the text of Zubiri) a relation
of communion, a "we" and not an "I." In the Greek and
Zubirian sense of personality, an isolated person would be
a metaphysical monstrosity. As pointed out in the first
chapter, person is less an incommunicability and a sealed
center as in Jacques Maritain than a communicability and
an open communion in the ecstasy of love. Nature is the
bond of unity between persons, that which is communi-
cated by father to son. The community of nature grows
out of the primacy of the ecstasy of personality. Therefore God, for the patristic mind as seen by Zubiri, is a personal and *hence* self-giving Action; this Act, an infinite
ecstasy and fecundity, is expressed within Himself in the
Trinity and beyond in the act of creation. The priority of
personality over nature caused the Greek Fathers to approach the mystery of the Holy Trinity from a point of
view which differs from that of the Latins. Whereas the
Latins, according to Zubiri, began with the Unity of the
Divine Nature and attempted to understand the Three
Persons in the light of that Unity, the Greeks began with
the Three Persons and saw the Unity of Nature in the light
of the Trinity of Persons.[55] Their eminently *personalistic*

theology was made possible by a theory of the real that
saw the ultimate meaning of being in agape, in ecstasy as
rooted precisely in God as personal, as superabundant.[56]

Agape and Being

WE ARE now in a position to apply the method that has
controlled Zubiri's investigation to his own conclusions:
that is, the plurality of *rationes entis* and their relation to
an order permitting a new *ratio* to "radicalize" an older
one. Beginning with a "cosmological" *ratio* of being as the
actualization of a potency, and therefore as something finished, complete, we are forced by the unfinished structure
of the being of human historicity to seek another *ratio*. We
find it in immanence, a kind of act that renews itself and
thus recapitulates the past. But this exercise of being as an
act leads us to being as ecstasy, as *eros*, being seeking its
own perfection. Still another *ratio*. But if finite being as
nature is *eros*, as personal it is agape. Agape culminates in
God, whose pure superabundance reveals itself from within
Trinitarian Life and from without in creation. This last
ratio forces us to radicalize our understanding of the finite
as *eros*. Pushing beyond the text of Zubiri but remaining, I
believe, faithful to his method, we can say that agape, although formally personal, is analogically present, even in
eros. If I give of myself to a bed of flowers and bring them
into full bloom, then they in time perfect *me*, give of their

fragrance and their beauty to my contemplation. If I care for my boat by caulking its bottom every season, my boat "takes care of me" when I go sailing. Thus there is an interchange between *eros* and agape which might indicate their absorption into a still higher *ratio entis*.

Here the metaphysics of a thus disengaged love meets Martin Heidegger's doctrine on the meaning of *techne*. According to Heidegger, the precise role of *techne*—as transcending mere technics while englobing them—is a knowledge

which puts into work the being of any particular essent. . . . The Greeks called art in the sense and the work of art *technē*, because art is what most immediately brings being (i.e. the appearing that stands there in itself) to stand, stabilizes it in a work, not primarily because it is wrought [*gewirkt*], made, but because it brings about [*er wirket*] being in an essent. . . . It is through the work of art as essent being that everything else that appears and is to be found is first confirmed and made accessible, explicable and understandable as being or not being.[57]

Art, fundamentally, "is the ability, pure and simple, to put-into-the-work (*ins-Werk-setzen*) . . . the manifesting realization of being *in* the essent." The opening of any reality into the fullness of its own being—be it a kingdom by a statesman or a garden by a housewife—is not only the work man accomplishes in the thing, but it is the understanding and contemplation, the joy, he takes in that thing itself. The opening of that reality through the work of man is both the perfection of that thing itself and, simultaneously, that thing's giving of itself to man. Being surrenders itself to a man who has surrendered himself to being. Man—speaking quite literally and with the full force of metaphysical language—is, as Heidegger insists, the place wherein being appears and shows itself. In turn, man who opens being to its fullness is he to whom being is thus opened. The Greeks knew this when they insisted that the truth of being *be spoken* by man. The early Christian Fathers knew this more profoundly when they insisted that creation share in redemption and that human history is a preparing of the cosmos for the Day of Glory. Without the spirit and hand of man, being is simply not perfected and without being man is not. The latter assertion demands further elucidation, but let us note well that the very structure of finite reality demands man for its own perfection and that this perfection is a dimension of the ecstatic structure of human existence.

In *Das Wesen der Wahrheit*, Heidegger speaks of Truth, of the truth of being, as a "letting-being-be." Without accepting all the implications of the Heideggerian position, we can agree that man possesses the truth of being when he stands before reality reverently and permits being to reveal itself. But this "standing before reality" must not be understood as though it were a passive contemplation of a work of art hung in a museum. Here Heidegger has transcended the Greek conception of contemplation as something of itself divorced from work. Being is "let-be" only when being has been brought forth "into-the-work." Being *be*-comes itself when man brings it into achievement or fullness. Thus the work wrought by a Toledo craftsman in steel brings that steel into the being of a tempered blade, a sword, that essence which was written into the steel as its very hope and destiny. The artisan has permitted being *to be* by working it into its perfection. This work is not something that lies exclusively within the artist. The actuality of the work has passed into the thing acted upon; that thing, in turn, in receiving the activity of the artist has been quickened and has been thus "set-into-the-work" of its own being, has become in act the sword that it hitherto was only in potency and as a promise. Being is "let be" only through the generosity of the work that man effects within its heart. If man is the place wherein being shows itself, it is because being's "showing of itself," being's unveiling of its own perfection, calls for the hand of the human spirit. Here the very contemplation of being requires the work of man. Here contemplation and action are united in the catalyst of reverence and love. In this eminently existential act, being is lifted into history. The Aristotelian overemphasis on the contemplative and the Reformation shift to the active represent typical ways in which the ontological balance and tension within existence can be disrupted by human freedom. The Catholic fusion of work and play, action and contemplation, prayer and deed, is an articulation of the very structure of being in its relationship to man.

Although I am thinking here primarily of man's relationship to what is not man, this analysis holds true in a supreme manner within man's relationship to man. The surrender of the lover to the beloved opens the beloved to her lover and thus to herself. The acceptance of love is thus the revelation to the beloved of her own being. The lover in loving becomes the voice of his beloved. The difference between this love of man for man, of man for woman, and the love which man gives the world, the work

he brings about within creation, is that the voice he gives
his beloved is *her* own, whereas the voice he gives the
world remains *his* own. And this voice, the perfection of a
universe singing to its master, both is and is not man. It is
not man in that man has brought the world into *its* very
own; it is man in that this perfection is the human hand
and soul in another order of being. It is man, finally, in that
the consciousness and love of this voice are man's and not
the world's. This is why the blessing of man by man is a
hope, whereas the blessing of the world by man is a
certainty.

The absorption of the being of the world into the ecstasy
of human existence conquers the alienation Ortega dis-
covers between the Eleatic and the immanent, between the
static and the dynamic. Man, by opening up the richness
of existence, permits all being *to be* its very fullness. This
fullness of being, its goodness, is "diffusive," in the language of Dionysius the Areopagite. As interpreted by
Aquinas, the diffusiveness of being is the actual perfecting
it operates within the heart of its lover. A being can truly
be, therefore, only when it is loved. Its state of being-
loved releases its agathonic character, and the restlessness
and self-centeredness of *eros*—written into the very dynamism of reality—now fuses with an agape borrowed from
agape.

It is precisely here that the speculations of both José
Ortega y Gasset and Xavier Zubiri might possibly move
Thomists to look more deeply into the meaning of being
they have inherited from St. Thomas Aquinas. Although
the dynamic and open character of the act of existing is
often stressed verbally in contemporary Thomism, some-

times one has the impression that this is so much tub thumping. The absence of any sophisticated attempt to meet both historicism and existentialism on their own grounds is one indication of what I mean. Another is the propensity to believe that some one concept of being— even if it be the privileged Cajetanian concept of a proportional unity within an absolute difference—yields the full meaning of being. But concepts of being are actually by-products of the metaphysician's attempt to come to grips with what it means to be. This meaning emerges very slowly in the career of a philosopher, and it emerges as a result of judgments and reasonings upon data which are as broad as being itself—data involving being as history as well as nature, being as power (for example, Tillich) as well as repose, being as ecstatic as well as perfected. In the light of the above, I will limit my concluding remarks in this chapter to two considerations which are the results of my having read and meditated the works of both Ortega and Zubiri: one looks to the inner structure of finite being, and the other concerns the "open" structure of Infinite as well as finite being.

Etienne Gilson has pointed up the tendency of Cajetan, repeated by many modern Thomists, to limit the role of existence to that of ultimate or final act in the order of being.[58] In this conception, existence is seen as the crown of being, its ratification so to speak. The fully individualized essence stands in potency to its act within the order of being. Existence, hence, is an act which is understood as being principally *received*, and yet limited in that very reception. Thomists who maintain that position are not so naïve as to imagine that the essence somehow waits in the

wings of the theater of being prior to its reception of existence. Nonetheless, they do see the fully constituted and
already existing nature as a potency, a receptacle, whose
final actualization is existence. I would suggest that lurking
within this conception of being is what both Ortega and
Zubiri have described as the "Eleatic" or static notion of
being. Bañez, centuries ago, had already told us that "to-
be-received-in-essence" is not the *ratio formalis* of the act
of being, even the act of being of the creature. If we
translate his Latin as "the full meaning of being," we can
say that if *esse* is received, it is certainly not received the
way in which a form is received in matter or the way in
which formal actuality is the actualization of a potency in
the order of operation. The meaning of being is deeper
than this. Cajetan's tendency to see existence as though it
were the final term of a process of change, of generation,
involved his seeing the act of being as something completed
and settled, finished, once it had been received. Although
he insisted upon the difference between "existence as sig-
nified" and "existence as exercised," existence became for
all speculative purposes nothing other than the empirical
factuality, the outside-of-its-causes, of a fully constituted
nature. But *esse*, according to St. Thomas, is not only that
by which being subsists outside its causes; *esse* is also that
by which being tends toward its end and rests in it once
found.[59]

The inner constitution of the act-potency relationship
as it emerges from the *esse*-essence relationship must not be
modeled upon a relationship proper to a potency which is
also a capability prior to its actuality. Before a white shirt
is dyed black its potency to be black is a real capacity, but

before a being exists *it* simply is not a capacity of any kind. Potency, in the order of essence, pre-exists its actuality and therefore *controls* that actuality and *limits it* "from without" (if I may be permitted the expression). This is what we might call the "Eleatic moment" within being, and it certainly is, as Ortega suggests, the moment of being that we *see* with the naked eye and feel with our hands.[60]

St. Thomas pointed to the radically unique structure of the *esse*-essence relationship in a famous text in the *De Potentia Dei* which Gilson has characterized as having itself reached the very limits of human langauge.[61] Aquinas, insisting that the act of existing gathers within itself all perfections and that this act is itself the perfection of perfections because the act of acts, lays down as a cardinal principle for understanding what *he* means by *esse* the following reversal of the Aristotelian formula: nothing could determine *esse* as an act determines a potency because beyond *esse* there is only nothing and nothing cannot determine. "Therefore *esse* is not determined by something as is a potency by an act, but rather as is an act by a potency." Gilson, in commenting upon the text, says that this turns upside down the usual formula in which act determines the plasticity of potency. "The essence of a finite act of existing consists in being *nothing more than* this or that *esse* . . . each essence is posited by an act of existing which is not the essence but which includes the essence as its own autodetermination."[62]

In different terms we might say that the essence-*esse* structure is a paradox. Essence is other than *esse*, but this "otherness" is not the otherness of opposition because the very *being* of the other—essence—is that of which it is other, *esse*. Essence, being the internal so-much of an *esse*, structures the *esse* it defines from within, but functions as this structure only because it is being through its own otherness, *esse*. This is the only ontological situation in which an "other" is set up within that of which it is other and *by that* of which it is other, precisely because its very being *is* that of which it is other!

Let us recall Ortega's insistence that the actuality of immanence is act as potency, an act which—through the repetition and prolongation of itself—renovates its own potency. This is an act which generates rather than destroys its own potency. Let us recall Zubiri's contention that being, in its deepest level, is ecstatic, a burgeoning outward of the inner riches of itself. If we situate these insights within the existential metaphysics of St. Thomas, they add a new meaning, a new *ratio* in Zubiri's language, to our understanding of what it means to be. In a purely Eleatic universe, the openness and ecstatic structure of the real must lie on the side of potency, not on the side of act. Potency, as a capability and as a plasticity, looks out upon a world of possibility that will be stamped upon itself and thus seal and close its own openness by an actuality. This is the world of Sartre wherein the infinite possibility of human freedom is restricted by choice, wherein the need to be free destroys the breadth which originally constituted man as that lone "X" without essence that fashions an essence by limiting and thus enslaving himself to the object of his choice. Let us not tarry over what might be valid in this conception, but simply emphasize the truth that within such a universe potency is the open door and act the closed door. But in a universe in which the potency of being is not determined but determines; in a universe in which act is the determined; in a universe in which the determining occurs from within the determined (*esse*), the open principle of the real will be act—*esse*—and the closed principle will be potency—essence. In this Thomistic universe the open and dynamic principle perfects the closed principle which functions as a limit. For this reason Domingo Bañez, another Spaniard, could say that the *less* essence found in a finite being, the more perfection there is to be found in that same being.[63] In this universe the openness of human history might well be the finest analogue of the Personal Agape of the Greater of both the natural world and of that adventure which the Spaniards are wont to call, after their Roman forefathers, the *rerum gestarum*.

Notes

1. For example, Rafael Calvo Serer, *España, sin problema* (Madrid: Ediciones Rialp, 1949); Manuel Garcia Morente, *Ideas para una filosofia de la historia de España* (Madrid: Ediciones Rialp, 1957); Antonio Millan Puelles, *Ontologia de la existencia histórica* (Madrid: Ediciones Rialp, 1956).

2. Juan Lopez Ibor, *El español y su complejo de inferioridad* (Madrid: Ediciones Rialp, 1955), p. 78.

3. Cf. the fine study by Eric Voegelin, *Order and History*, Vol. 2, *The World of the Polis* (Baton Rouge: Louisiana State University Press, 1957).

4. Juan Lopez Ibor, *El descubrimiento de la intimidad* (Madrid, 1958), pp. 19–28.

5. For example, Rafael Gambra Ciudad, *Eso se llama el estado* (Seville, 1958).

6. Rafael Calvo Serer, *Politica de integración* (Madrid, 1950); *La configuración del futuro* (Madrid, 1952).

7. José Ortega y Gasset, *Historia como sistema*, 3 edición en

castillano (Madrid: Revista de Occidente, 1958). Although a fine English edition exists, it is not available to me here in Baghdad, where I am writing.

8. *Ibid., passim.*

9. *Ibid.,* p. 28.

10. *Ibid.,* p. 30.

11. Xavier Zubiri, *Naturaleza, Historia, Dios* (Madrid: Editora Nacional, 1959), pp. 143–183.

12. Ortega, *op. cit.,* p. 44.

13. *Ibid.*

14. *Ibid.,* p. 45.

15. *Ibid.,* p. 47.

16. *Ibid.,* p. 48.

17. *Ibid.,* p. 48.

18. *Ibid.,* p. 50–51.

19. *Ibid.,* p. 56.

20. *Ibid.,* pp. 122–140. Ortega principally uses the following texts: *De Anima*, 417, b. 3; *Metaphysics*, Book IX, 1048 b. 18–1049 b. 34. (The following pages claim to be nothing more than an exegesis of Ortega on Aristotle, and should not be read as an exegesis of the Aristotelian text itself.)

21. *Ibid.,* p. 126.

22. *Ibid.,* p. 128.

23. *Ibid.*

24. Aristotle, *Physics*, III, 201 b. 33.

25. Ortega, *op. cit.,* p. 130.

26. *Ibid.,* p. 130–131.

27. *Ibid.,* p. 131.

28. *Ibid.,* p. 132. Italics added.

29. *Ibid.,* p. 133.

30. *Ibid.*

31. It might be objected against Ortega that he fails to distinguish between potency as capability and potency as limit. The objection would not damage Ortega's main point and, besides, Aristotle himself did not conceive of potency as a limit. Cf. W. Norris Clarke, "The Limitation of Act by Potency," *The New Scholasticism*, Vol. XXVI, No. 2 (1952), pp. 178–183.

32. Ortega, *op. cit.,* p. 134.

33. *Ibid., passim.*

34. *Ibid.*, p. 136.

35. *Ibid.*, p. 133.

36. *Ibid.*, p. 137.

37. Since Zubiri is almost totally unknown to the Anglo-Saxon world despite his pre-eminence in Spain and despite the translation of much of his work into French, it might be wise to detail something of his life. Born in San Sebastian, December 4, 1898, he received his doctor's degree in theology in Rome (1920) and his degree in philosophy in Madrid (1921). During his very early career he pioneered in the phenomenology of judgment. Sometime professor of the history of philosophy at the University of Madrid, he has also taught at the University of Barcelona. A man of vast erudition, Zubiri studied philosophy with Zaragüeta, Ortega, Hüsserl, and Heidegger; physics and mathematics with La Vallée-Poussin in Louvain, with Rey Pastor y Palacios in Madrid, with Zermelo in Freiburg, with Schrödinger in Berlin, and with Louis de Broglie in Paris; biology with Noyons and van Gehuchten in Louvain, with Spemann in Freiburg, with Goldschmidt and Mangold in Berlin; oriental languages and ancient history with P. Deimel in Rome, and with Labat, Benveniste, Dherme and Delaporte in Paris. Zubiri came to philosophy with a theological background and a profound, although unobtrusive, Catholicity sustains his thought—a Catholicity that reaches its height in his meditation upon the meaning of Pauline thought in his *Naturaleza, Historia, Dios.* Neither the founder of a school nor the member of a school, Zubiri has been influenced by both medieval and existentialist thought, yet it would be inaccurate to call him either a scholastic or an existentialist.

38. Zubiri, *Naturaleza, Historia, Dios,* p. 288. For a fine study of Zubiri on history, cf. Louis Diez del Corral, "Zubiri y la filosofia de la Historia," in *Homenaje a Xavier Zubiri* (Madrid, 1953), pp. 69–89.

39. Zubiri, *op. cit.,* p. 297.

40. Martin Heidegger, *Sein und Zeit* (Tübingen: Niemeyer, 1952), pp. 214 ff.

41. The doctrine has heavily influenced contemporary existential analysis. Cf. Rollo May, Ernest Angel, Henri F. Ellenberger, eds., *Existence: A New Dimension in Psychiatry and Psychology* (New York: Basic Books, 1958).

42. It is quite clear why Karl Löwith is correct in his contention

that the supposedly arbitrary handling of philosophical texts by
Heidegger grows out of his understanding of the role of the past in
the economy of man's life. If answers make sense only in terms of
the questions I ask and if these questions grow out of my concern
for the future, then the past must structure itself according to the
questions I put to it. K. Löwith, *Heidegger: Ein Denker in dürftiger
Zeit* (Frankfurt: Fischer, 1953). A similar presupposition lies behind Eric Voegelin's *Order and History*, Vol. 1, *Israel and Revelation* (Baton Rouge: Louisiana State University Press, 1956). Cf. my
own study, "Israel and Revelation," *Modern Age*, Vol. 3, No. 2
(Spring 1959), pp. 182–189.

43. Zubiri, *op. cit.*, p. 325.

44. A similar doctrine, reached from different presuppositions,
can be found in Bernard J. F. Lonergan, *Insight: A Study of Human Understanding* (New York: Longmans, Green, 1957), pp.
348–375.

45. Zubiri, *op. cit.*, pp. 315–332.

46. *Ibid.*, chapter entitled "El ser sobrenatural: Dios y la dei-
ficación en la teología paulina," pp. 341–409.

47. *Ibid.*, p. 350.

48. *Ibid.*, p. 351.

49. The above analysis is taken from *ibid.*, "El Ser de Dios," pp.
348–362.

50. *Ibid.*, pp. 352–353. Unlike Ortega, Zubiri is willing to find a
dynamic conception of being in Plato, but it is evident that he considers it less important than the Aristotelian conception. Concerning the dialectic between Platonism and Aristotelianism, Zubiri has
the following interesting observation: "El aspecto activo (del ser)
de Aristóteles quedó a veces soterrado bajo el actualista, y por
singular paradoja lo más rico del pensar aristotélico sobrevivió tan
sólo asociado al platonismo. Así se explica que San Juan Damasceno,
oficialmente aristotélico, se encuentre identificado con los pensa-
dores de raigambre más platónica, precisamente por haber recogido
con tacto esta pureza activa de la *enérgeia*. En cambio, los llambdos
aristotélicos absorbieron cada vez más la idea platónico en el 'con-
cepto' aristotélico. Esta indica, dicho sea de paso, que el estudio del
neoplatonismo es uno de los tres o cuatro temas más urgentes de la
historia de la filosofia antigua" (*ibid.*, p. 354).

51. *Ibid.*, p. 353.

52. *Ibid.*, pp. 355–357.

53. For an evaluation of Zubiri's relation to theology, cf. Augusto A. Ortega, "Zubiri y la Teologia," in *Homenaje a Xavier Zubiri*, pp. 179–193.

54. Zubiri, *op. cit.*, p. 359.

55. Zubiri's meditation upon the Holy Trinity and man's deification is the culmination of his study, but we abstract from considering it formally here because of the specifically philosophical nature of this essay. Nonetheless, the following passage is a résumé of Zubiri's position: "Los latinos, siguiendo la ruta trazada por San Agustín, parten de la unidad de Dios. . . . su problema estriba en concebir la trinidad de personas . . . sin mengua de esta unidad primaria. Los griegos, en cambio, . . . trataron de entender la índole de cada persona, y su problema estriba en concebir cómo esas tres personas sean sólo una misma cosa. Esta diferencia de actitud viene implicada ya en su concepte del ser y de la persona. Los latinos propendieron a ver en Dios, ante todo, una naturaleza a la que nada falta, y que, por consiguiente, tiene racionalidad, y, por tanto, personalidad. Los griegos ven en Dios, ante todo, una persona que en cierto modo se realiza en su propia naturaleza. El resultado será claro. Los latinos verán en Dios una sola naturaleza que subsiste en tres personas; distintas por su relación de origen, las personas ante todo se oponen. Los griegos verán más bien cómo Dios al realizarse como persona se tripersonaliza, de tal suerte que la trinidad de personas es justamente la manera metafísica de tener una naturaleza idéntica; las personas no comienzan por openerse, sino por implicarse y reclamarse en su respectiva distinción. Mientras para los latinos cada persona *está* en la otra en el sentido de que las tres tienen una naturaleza numéricamente idéntica, para los griegos cada persona no puede existir sino *produciendo* la otra, y del concurso de esta producción personal queda asegurada (si se me permite la expresión) la idéntica naturaleza de un solo Dios. Para los griegos, la trinidad es el modo misterioso de ser un Dios infinito, uno por naturaleza. Para los latinos, la trinidad es el modo misterioso cómo las unidad subsiste en tres personas" (*ibid.*, pp. 363–4).

56. The ecstatic notion of being has a long tradition in Spanish thought. Blessed Ramon Lull, often accused of having tried to prove rationally the existence of the Trinity, really said something rather more subtle: once you have granted that God is *Father* and

once you have seen that being is diffusive of itself, then the Trinity follows rationally. (Thus the Father is *unicus, magnificus, bonificans*, etc.; the Son is *unitum, magnificatum, bonificatum*, etc.; the Spirit is *unire, magnificare*, etc.: *Vita Beati Raymundi Lulli*, P. I & II, la.; *Liber de Confirmatione legis Christianae*, MS., f.205v–206, de maj. fine; *Hamar*, 11–11A.) Without endorsing the obvious excesses of Lull, it is interesting to note that his exasperation with his Islamic antagonist, Alim Hamar, grows out of the latter's failure to grant any expansive and diffusive meaning to being: the Being of God, for Hamar, is locked within the sterility of a Unity that would *lose itself* were it to expand into Trinitarian Life, whereas the Unity of the Christian God *is* Unity precisely in being Trinity, maintained Lull. The personalism of the Spanish philosopher in our time has been aptly expressed by Chesterton's "To us God Himself is a society. . . . For it is not well for God to be alone" (*Orthodoxy* [London and New York: John Lane, 1909], pp. 251–252).

57. Martin Heidegger, *An Introduction to Metaphysics*, trans. by Ralph Manheim (New Haven: Yale University Press, 1959), p. 159.

58. Etienne Gilson, "Cajetan et l'existence," *Tijdschrift voor Philosophie*, Vol. 15 (1953), pp. 267–286.

59. *De Veritate*, Q. 21, a. 2; "cum eiusdem rationis sit tendere in finem, et in fine quodammodo quiescere. . . . Haec autem duo inveniuntur competere ipsi esse."

60. Of course, neither the eye nor the hand nor any sense power knows being, but the intelligence can fashion—and has done so, as indicated—a theory of being that fits reality as we sense it and that ignores reality as we *experience* it.

61. *De Potentia Dei*, Q. VII, a. 2, ad. 9: "Nec intelligendum est quod ei quod dico *esse*, aliquid addatur quod sit eo formalius, ipsum determinans sicut actus potentiam; *esse* enim quod hujusmodi est, est aliud secundum essentiam ab eo cui additur determinandum. Nihil autem potest addi ad *esse* quod sit extraneum ab eo, cum ab eo nihil sit extraneum nisi non ens, quod non potest esse nec forma nec materia. Unde non sic determinatur *esse* per aliud sicut potentia per actum, sed magis sicut actus per potentiam." Gilson's commentary, the best I know on the text, is in his *Le Thomisme, Introduction à la philosophie de saint Thomas d'Aquin*, 5me édition revue et augmentée (Paris: Librarie Philosophique J. Vrin, 1944), p. 54. The more recently revised English version is not available to me here in

Iraq. See Etienne Gilson, *The Christian Philosophy of St. Thomas Aquinas,* trans. by I. T. Eschmann, O.P. (New York: Random House, 1956).

62. Gilson, *op. cit.,* p. 54.

63. Domingo Bañez, *Schol. Com., o.c. 3, 4, col. 224/C.* (Salamanca, 1585).

III

Non-Being, Power, and Love

Paul Tillich: Being as the Power to Be

THE PRIMACY of the ecstatic and agathonic within being has been challenged in our time by Paul Tillich, who sees being principally as a tragedy conquered by self-affirmation and courage, by what he eloquently calls "the power to be." The ontology of Tillich not only illustrates the division between the Protestant world which has emphasized the tragic sense of life, and the Catholic world which has given the primacy to agape, but it also points up relations between love and power that are consubstantial with a metaphysics of ecstasy. If I turn to an analysis of the thought of the Protestant theologian, I do not do so principally to take objection to what he holds, but to learn from him. By a singular paradox, those insights of mine which have lead me to differ from Tillich would never have been possible had I not gone to school through the reading of his own system.

Paul Tillich concluded his Terry Foundation Lectures, *The Courage to Be*, with this now famous sentence: "The courage to be is rooted in the God who appears when God has disappeared in the anxiety of doubt."[1] When God is no longer the Reality of a Presence and not even the outline of a conviction, when the soul—seeking this God who has forsaken it—passes beyond itself and there in the void confronts the horror of an absence absolute and unconditional, the soul can be said to have cracked the boundaries of being. Beyond there is only nothing. Nothing cannot speak to man and the only human response to this awful silence is anxiety. But by taking anxiety into himself, by affirming the meaning of his own confrontation with meaninglessness, man asserts himself against the void. Such a man, according to Tillich, has the courage to be. Within him, one with the very being he is, is the power to be against the darkness closing round him. "The source of this affirmation of meaning within meaninglessness," maintains Tillich, "is the 'God of God,' the power of being, which works through those who have no name for it, not even the name of God."[2]

Affirming himself against the nothing which fills the mask of all evil, doubting his own doubt, despairing and despairing of his own despair, the man broken under the wheel of anxiety thus affirms his own being because his being is a *being-in-despair*. Here is a meaning which has passed beyond every ethical distinction, a meaning which in truth fingers the roots of reality itself. Tillich warns his readers against building a doctrine upon such an extreme anxiety, but he concludes by observing that these end situations are criteria by which the truth of any theological system can be tested.[3] This last is a truth so simple that no Christian could seriously deny it. If Christ passed through the desolation of knowing Himself abandoned by His own Father, if Christ

upon the Cross bore the sufferings of all men, therefore
Christ is He who suffers the anguish of any man murdered
upon the wheel of despair. A theology that cannot speak to
such a man does not merit the title of Christian. Here the
Christian vision of the Catholic G. K. Chesterton, in some
ways so utterly opposed to that of the Protestant, meets the
insights of Paul Tillich:

But in that terrific tale of the Passion there is a distinct emotional suggestion that the author of all things (in some unthink-
able way) went not only through agony, but through doubt.
. . . He passed in some superhuman manner through our human
horror of pessimism. When the world shook and the sun was
wiped out of heaven, it was not at the crucifixion, but at the
cry from the cross: the cry which confessed that God was forsaken of God . . . let the atheists themselves choose a God.
They will find only one divinity who ever uttered their isolation; only one religion in which God for an instant seemed to
be an atheist.[4]

Paul Tillich's teaching of the God beyond the God of
theism "takes seriously the radical doubt experienced by
many people. It gives one the courage of self-affirmation
even in the extreme state of radical doubt. In such a state
the God of both religious and theological language disappears. But something remains, namely, the seriousness of
that doubt in which meaning within meaninglessness is affirmed."[5]

Pressing into the service of Protestantism the weight of
the phenomenological method; utilizing with the delicacy
of an artist the latest discoveries of existential analysis; sensi-
tive to the meaning of the contemporary preoccupation

with symbolism and mythology; open to the broken world of today, Tillich has concentrated the whole into a vision of Christian existence in the midst of human tragedy that has no parallel in our time. Tillich's system, which takes into its heart the profound doubt that has secularized half the Western world, is exactly what it claims to be: a latter-day apologetic conceived by a man who would be all things to all men in the tradition of St. Paul.

I have no intention of discussing the theology of Paul Tillich as such. Whether or not he has reduced the substance of Christianity to existential ontology, as the Barthians maintain, is an issue from which I abstract both by the economy of this study and by my reluctance to enter a dialectic belonging properly to the Protestant world, a world not my own. But no philosopher who attempts to probe the meaning of being in our day can afford to neglect Tillich's contributions to the ontology of existence. Theologically, Tillich's ontology is strictly functional, a handmaid to his theology.[6] In this, Tillich is strongly traditional and there are parallels between his conception of the role of philosophy in theology and the conception entertained by the great masters of the Middle Ages. But just as we can isolate the metaphysics that function within Thomism and Scotism from their properly theological context, so can we do the same for the ontology of Tillich. That this task ought to be done, for the sake of theology as well as for that of philosophy, is suggested by the temper of Tillich's mind which implies that there is a properly ontological intuition at the heart of Protestantism dividing it from Catholicism.[7]

This Protestant intuition locates the meaning of being in

its power, in its dynamic and active affirmation of itself
against the forces of darkness and the negativities that sur-
round all life. In turn, Tillich insists that whereas the
power of being marks the Protestant mind, love as an ecstasy has always held supremacy within the Catholic
world.[8] He refers explicitly to the great mystical tradition
within Catholic Christianity, but he might with equal justice have referred to the Baroque world of the seventeenth
century, which Dawson, utilizing the language of Sombart,
has called an "erotic" age.[9] Without delaying here over
what we might call, after Xavier Zubiri, the ontological
"horizon" within which Protestantism and Catholicism
function as styles of being, as ways of life within history,
we must be struck nonetheless by the possibilities for metaphysics that Tillich opens up for us. If Zubiri is correct in
his contention that there is a primacy of love within being
in the metaphysics of the Eastern Catholic tradition; if
Dawson is correct in saying that the whole Baroque Age is
ecstatic; and if Tillich is correct in his contention that
power holds the primacy within the Protestant mind, then
it would follow that a properly ontological penetration of
the issue would do a service not only to theology but to
the philosophy of culture as well. The study that follows,
while strictly philosophical in method and structure, nonetheless has in mind an end which is both theological and
cultural, an end which I trust will emerge gradually as a
result of the ontological analysis undertaken.

In his *The Courage to Be*, as well as in *Love, Power,
and Justice*, Tillich moves immediately to an analysis of
what he considers to be the basic ontological dialectic, the
dialectic between being and non-being; but his analysis of

the meanings of existence found in Volume II of his *Systematic Theology* provides the best introduction to his ontology. Words such as "existence," says Tillich, cannot be shriveled to a nominalistic universe because "words are the results of the encounter of the human mind with reality."[10] It follows that words are not merely conventional signs but are also symbols. Were this not true, "new languages would continuously have had to be invented in the fields of religion and the humanities."[11] The recovery of the true meaning of ontological and theological terms is a task which is one with these disciplines themselves. For Tillich the symbol differs from the sign in that the sign simply points to the reality it signifies without bearing any intrinsic relation to it.[12] The symbol, on the contrary, partakes of what it signifies and draws the man symbolizing into a lived relation with the symbolized. (Tillich advances the medieval and early modern symbol of the crown as a vivid example of what he means.) The symbol *has* or possesses the truth of the symbolized and for this reason the symbol *is* true. The dialectic between symbol and symbolized resembles Kierkegaard's subjective as opposed to objective truth. In an objective truth relation the mind is drawn to the reality known, and the subject disappears, so to speak, before the known reality which appears objectively in the disappearance of the subjectivity of the subject. A mathematician could not care less about his personal relations to triangularity; his business as a mathematician is to make the triangle appear before the mind, understanding as an anonymous observer understands. This is the mind as a knowing function common to all men. But in a subjective truth relation the whole person is drawn to the reality known precisely to the degree to which the person himself *is re-lated*. The more I plunge into the other, the more I plunge into myself because the relation is one involving my very subjectivity *as related to the other*. According to Tillich, philosophy is a dialectic of attachment and detachment, a tension between the person knowing and the reality known.[13] Neither pole of the tension can be dissolved, and the tension is mediated by the living symbol which leads man into a participation with ultimate reality.

The word "existence" is such a symbol. Asserting that "etymological inquiries indicate directions" although "they do not solve problems,"[14] Tillich points out that "the root meaning of 'to exist,' is Latin *existere*, is 'to stand out.' "[15] In English this "standing out" is the common characteristic of all things whereby they "stand outside of" non-being or nothingness. But Greek philosophical vocabulary lends a precious refinement to this "standing outside" non-being. "Nonbeing can be understood in two ways, namely, as *ouk on*, that is, absolute nonbeing, or as *me on*, that is, relative nonbeing."[16] "Standing out" of something implies that the thing is standing "in" something. All things stand in their own being as opposed to absolute non-being (*ouk on*), but they stand in their own being as opposed also to relative non-being (*me on*) to the degree to which they are actualized, to the degree to which they exercise the "power of being." To the extent to which something is not the fullness of itself, to the extent to which it is dynamically moving toward a plenitude of being hitherto unpossessed, it both "stands in" and "out of" relative non-being.

These etymological pointers lead us to the existentialist problem, says Tillich:

Within the whole of being as it is encountered, there are structures which have no existence and things which have existence on the basis of structures. Treehood does not exist, although it has being, namely, potential being. But the tree in my back yard does exist. It stands out of the mere potentiality of treehood. But it stands out and exists only because it participates in that power of being which is treehood, that power which makes every tree a tree and nothing else.[17]

The religious symbol of "the Fall" points to the ontological split between man's essential and existential being. "There is no existential gap in the myth of the Fall. In existence, man is what he is in essence . . . the bearer of critical and constructive reason . . . the maker of himself as the actualization of his potentiality."[18] This is man not only as expressed in the myth of the Fall, but it is also the man of the Renaissance and the Enlightenment, man as essentially and existentially good. Existentialism was able to insert itself into modern thought precisely because this image of man does not correspond to human nature as we find it in reality. Forever falling into sin, menaced by sickness and evil, the prey to fate and fortune, man hurtles forward through history, a comet whose life is burnt out in the ashes of the past, and a creature whose only absolute future is the curtain of death. Such is man after the Fall. The Fall, for Tillich, does not represent an event that preceded history, but it is rather a structure encountered *within* history forming part of the very constitution of existing humanity. Expressed in ontological rather than theological language, man is always estranged from his essential being. This estrangement forms human existence into a tension between being and non-being in all its "forms." Existence, therefore, is inserted within being as a structure partaking of essence as well as existence itself ("existence" here meaning the factual "being *there*" of a thing). Broadening the use of the term, as does Tillich himself, we can say that existence is the situation in which we encounter our being as well as our non-being, ourselves as standing inside and outside of being. God, in whom there is no estrangement, transcends the essence-existence polarity.[19]

The doctrine has enormous consequences in the system of Tillich, but before these consequences can be explored justly we must look to what the eminent German-American theologian means by being. There is a consistency to Tillich's teaching which runs through *The Courage To Be; Love, Power, and Justice;* and the *Systematic Theology* absolving the critic from approaching Tillich chronologically on this issue. Statements made about being in any of these studies complement and flesh out the doctrine found in the other books. The highly technical approach of the *Theology* lies behind the simple language of the *Love, Power, and Justice*, and both of them are seen in psychological and historical depth when read in the light of *The Courage To Be*.

Paul Tillich sees the whole of ontology summed up "in the simple and infinitely difficult question: What does it mean *to be?*"[20] The answer to this question is one with an analysis of "the structures common to everything that is, to everything that participates in being." *Pari passu*, these structures involve the historicity of man. Against the critics who believe that an ontology located within the context of history would dissolve man into the stream of change and thus destroy the universality of science, Tillich counters with the affirmation that, whereas the history of man essentially involves change, historicity as a structure *common* to men everywhere permits an ontological penetration.[21] Ontology always comes into being as a discipline as a result of man's historical confrontation with the real. As man experiences the real so will he articulate his understanding of being. His articulation will be true in proportion to his participation in the fullness of being and its ground. The symbols with which he expresses this participation will retain their force and hence their truth as long as man experiences being in *this* given way involving *these* given symbols. While there is no experimental way of verifying ontological judgments, there is an experiential way. This "is the way of an intelligent recognition of the basic ontological structures within the encountered reality, including the process of encountering itself. The only answer, but a sufficient one, which can be given to the question of ontological verification is the appeal to intelligent recognition."[22] If the ontological judgments fit reality as I encounter it, then they have all the validity I can expect from them. If these judgments fail to square themselves with reality as experienced, then either the system itself is faulty theoretically or the symbols motivating the judgments have lost their power. In that case, I would have ceased to live being in the old way and would have to set about articulating a new ontology in the light of my new encounter with existence. The interweaving of the subjective and the objective within this ontology could not be more clearly evidenced than in this epistemology.

The question of being is prompted by what Tillich calls "the shock of nonbeing."[23] This shock resembles Jacques Maritain's "intuition of Being,"[24] a privileged vision granted the man open to the treasures of being, and it also resembles Gabriel Marcel's "puzzlement over being." But whereas Maritain's intuition results in an analogical concept of being, whereas Marcel's puzzlement involves a kind of circling activity in which the philosopher approaches the mystery of being first from this and then from that angle, Tillich's "shock" formulates itself in the question, What does it mean to be? Despite his debt to Heidegger, Tillich does not see this fundamental question as being one with the famous "Why is there something? Why not Nothing?"[25] "This form of the question points to something that precedes being, from which being can be derived. But being can only be derived from being . . . being is the original fact which cannot be derived from anything."[26] But although the ontological question does not presume a nothing which would lie underneath being as does a carpet (one is reminded of Bergson's famous critique of the concept of non-being), the question is primed by a shock in which the negative side of the mystery of being—its abysmal element—is experienced. The possibility of non-being, borne in upon men by anxiety or by any one of a number of encounters with death and negativity, jars the mind out of its accustomed routine and faces it with the mystery of being. Although not produced by the *concept* of non-being as by an intelligibility anterior to being, the question about being is primed by a vision which involves a positive and a negative element: negatively, I experience the possibility of non-being, probably my own; positively, I experience the splendor of being, probably my own.

This experience of being in its positive sense is what the existential analysts try to produce in those of their patients for whom being has become trivial, a seemingly endless boredom, a continuum with neither meaning nor depth. This is being for Camus' *The Stranger*, for example. The re-birth of being within the human person, which precedes all ontology according to Tillich, has never been better expressed, in my opinion, than by a patient of Dr. Rollo May's, whose written account of her experience is recorded in that author's compilation, *Existence:*

I remember walking that day under the elevated tracks in a slum area, feeling the thought, "I am an illegitimate child." I recall the sweat pouring forth in my anguish in trying to accept that fact. Then I understood what it must feel like to accept, "I am a Negro in the midst of privileged whites," or "I am blind in the midst of people who see." Later on that night I woke up and it came to me this way, "I accept the fact that I am an illegitimate child." *But* "I am not a child anymore." So it is, "I am illegitimate." That is not so either: "I was born illegitimate." Then what is left? What is left is this, "*I Am.*" This *act* of contact and acceptance with "I am," once gotten hold of, gave me (what I think was for me the first time) the experience "Since I am, I have the right to be."

What is this experience like? It is a primary feeling—it feels like receiving the deed to my house. It is the experience of my own aliveness not caring whether it turns out to be an ion or just a wave. It is like when a very young child I once reached the core of a peach and cracked the pit, not knowing what I would find and then feeling the wonder of finding the inner seed, good to eat in its bitter sweetness. . . . It is like a sailboat in the harbor being given an anchor so that, being made out of earthly things, it can by means of its anchor get in touch again with the earth, the ground from which its wood grew; it can lift its anchor to sail but always at times it can cast its anchor to weather the storm or rest a little. . . . It is my saying to Descartes, "*I AM, therefore* I think, I feel, I do."

It is like an axiom in geometry—never experiencing it would be like going through a geometry course not knowing the first axiom. It is like going into my very own Garden of Eden where I am beyond good and evil and all other human contacts. It is like the experience of the poets of the intuitive world, the mystics, except that instead of the pure feeling of and union with God it is the feeling of and the union with my own being. It is like owning Cinderella's shoe and looking all over the world for the foot it will fit and realizing all of a sudden that one's own foot is the only one it will fit. . . . It is like a child in grammar finding the *subject* of the verb in a sentence—in this case the subject being one's own life span. It is ceasing to feel like a theory toward one's self. . . .[27]

Such an experience is an "ecstasy," according to Tillich, in which the mind "is grasped by the mystery, namely, by the ground of being and meaning."[28] From such an ecstasy emerges "all genuine philosophy."[29] But although an ecstasy, the experience—at least according to Tillich—is shot through and through with the shock of non-being, a shock that was too much for the early Greek philosophers. Unable to bear the face of nothingness, they tried to block it out by banishing non-being from rational discourse. But if we remain faithful to the experience of change and of age and death, we are forced to confront the relations between non-being and being. According to Tillich, there are two ways in which philosophy has tried to elucidate the question. One of these is logical and the other is ontological.

There are philosophical systems which attempt to reduce the problem of non-being to the logic of negation. Within these systems non-being is simply the role than denial plays within judgment. Ultimately non-being becomes the *kind of being* that a predicate exercises in a subject when that predicate is denied the subject. Here non-being is little more than a creature fashioned by the mind which, because a creation of the mind, is actually a kind of being itself.[30]

But logical negation, insists our author, must itself be rooted in an ontological situation if it is to be more than "merely a play with possible relations."[31] The judgment, "The soup was not served on time," involves the prior possibility of the soup's having been served on time, and it also involves the soup's being a kind of being that does not always live up to what is expected of it. Behind the negation there lies the ontological structure of the real, a structure involving non-being. Reality, therefore, is a dialectic englobing both being and non-being. Non-being, itself intelligible only in the light of being, enters into a living relation with being and forms existence into a perpetual Yes and No.

Here we move into the heart of Tillich's understanding of the meaning of being. Being, taken merely as an absolutely logical meaning, must totally exclude non-being. In turn, an absolute non-being would exclude being. In both instances the whole world, the totality of all the things that are, would be excluded. A world which is diversified, limited, structured and therefore finite, is a world in which relative or me-ontic non-being enters as the dialectical

otherness to being. The contingent fact of existence, revealed all too tragically in death as the dialectical consequence of having come into being, looks back upon the me-
ontic non-being out of which it has emerged and into the
me-ontic non-being toward which it hurtles in this its brief
span of "standing within being." For Tillich the being of
existence is implicated inexorably in the non-being from out
of which ex-istence stands. If being is a frozen and empty
meaning apart from non-being; if being actually does involve its own estrangement and alienation; if being must be
conceived and symbolized dialectically, then we are forced
to ask Tillich what is the law of the dialectic? How can we
conceive it? If he answered that the dialectic was simply the
law of being, he would have substituted a tautology for an
explanation. Quite obviously the dialectic *is* the law of being (on Tillich's assumptions), but our recognition of this
truth does not move us very far in our attempt to penetrate
the meaning of being. This meaning must be still further
symbolized and conceptualized, and Tillich does it for us
with the symbol of power. Being is its own power to be.[32]

Seeking the roots of the meaning of being deeply within
the Western tradition, within the Stoics, Tillich finds this
meaning first articulated with sophistication by Spinoza,
who taught that being was a conatus, a force, a power
through which each thing preserved itself in existence.[33]
Expanding this tradition within the context of contemporary existentialism, Tillich maintains that in the real world
being is always something *encountered* and this encounter
involves the negation of non-being. In an abstract world being would simply stare across a logical vacuum at its opposite, non-being. But in the real world man affirms his be-

ing by way of a negation of non-being, thus sealing his
identity against the void:

> We could not even think "being" without a double negation:
> being must be thought of as the negation of the negation of
> being. . . . This is why we describe being best by the metaphor
> "power of being." . . . The self-affirmation of being without
> nonbeing would not even be self-affirmation but an immovable
> self-identity. Nothing would be manifest, nothing expressed,
> nothing revealed. But nonbeing drives being out of its seclu-
> sion, it forces it to affirm itself dynamically.[34]

Being, therefore, is the cross formed by two nothings and is
that restless and dynamic center which erupts from out of
the intersection of this double negation. Being as a power
or as self-affirmation thus involves two moments, the Yes
and No of the dialectic, the Yes said to being is simultaneously the No said to non-being. Being is thus truly the negation of a negation; but whereas the second negation—the
non-being reacted against and resisted—is the enemy to being, the first negation—the positive resistance to non-being
—is the power of being itself, its center, heart, and ultimate
meaning.

The ethics of courage are themselves a manifestation of
the ontology of power, and it follows, says Tillich, that
man most truly asserts himself as being in and through a
courage which conquers anxiety by taking it within himself. The entire *The Courage to Be* is given over to the defense and elucidation of this thesis. The more non-being can
enter into being whereby it can be resisted and negated, the
more can being manifest itself and show forth its power.
For this reason God is best symbolized as the very ground

of being, the Power who conquers the very night of non-being by affirming Himself as absolute being in an absolutely infinite way against an absolute void of nothingness. In God, the Ground of Being itself, the distinction between me-ontic and ouk-ontic non-being is transcended by a Power whose Infinite Weight is such that it can crush out all non-being, even to the creation of the world out of nothing and to the conquest of the grave itself in a resurrection that promises an absolute victory over the powers of deat`. and annihilation.

Paul Tillich: The Primacy of Power Within Protestantism

EARLIER I pointed out that Paul Tillich's ontology is both eminently historical and eminently apologetic. By the first statement I meant that Tillich sees ontological formulations as taking place within a concrete historical situation that shapes these very formulations. By the second statement I mean that Tillich's ontology is elaborated for the sake of Protestant theology, a theology which is Christian and therefore historical. The ontology of Tillich illuminates the historical soil from which it is drawn and this soil in turn illuminates the ontology. Tillich, therefore, confronts the meaning of being and the meaning of history within a single context: in doing so he addresses himself to the two mysteries most troubling the philosophical mind today.

This union of a historical theology and a historical ontology permits Tillich to draw a number of conclusions which are crucial to the argument of this entire study: Tillich teaches that Protestantism, in giving the primacy within being to power, has reached a deeper level of authenticity and meaning in its confrontation with reality than has Catholicism, which has always given the primacy to love.

Accepting Tillich's statement of the facts as historically true (that is, power *does* have the primacy within the Protestant and love within the Catholic world), the strictly metaphysical issue nonetheless remains debatable: that is, is it really true that the conception of being as power is the deepest meaning of being? Does power in fact exercise a primacy over love within being? If Tillich is wrong metaphysically, then he must be wrong theologically. This, of course, would not argue either for the falsity of Protestantism or the truth of Catholicism. From a purely logical point of view, it would indicate merely that Tillich had badly conceptualized the Protestant experience. The issue is more dialectical than philosophical and I raise it simply to emphasize that what follows in this essay is a study in metaphysics and not in theology or sociology. Metaphysics, however, does have theological and cultural implications. The issue is further heightened in that Tillich's contention that an ontology of love is at the root of the Catholic experience of being agrees perfectly with Xavier Zubiri's conclusion that the primacy of agape is far more firmly fixed within the Catholic tradition than many Catholic philosophers themselves are aware. It also adds metaphysical depth to the thesis of Christopher Dawson that the Catholic Baroque was an ecstatic civilization thrown up in protest against the Protestant mercantile world of the North. The fact that the Catholic tradition in large part has rejected any static or Eleatic understanding of being—as has Tillich himself—renders a dialogue possible, a dialogue that might well deepen our understanding of being.

Tillich's appropriation of the ontology of power to the Protestant tradition enriches that very ontology, as I have indicated. It is therefore instructive to watch Tillich link being as the courage to be with Luther's "courage of confidence" and with the Lutheran understanding of faith. It is equally instructive to watch him apply the dialectic of being and non-being to the theology of the Trinity. These two issues, more than any other, heighten our appreciation of Tillich's ontology, and face it all the more sharply with metaphysical traditions that have grown out of a soil that has always sensed being as something other than the power to be, a soil alien to historic Protestantism.

Just as the ethics of courage can be understood truly only in the light of the power of being, so too can the dynamics of faith be grasped only in terms of the same ontological structure. Faith, teaches Tillich, while articulating itself in a conscious religious act in which man accepts his own acceptance by the Ground of Being from whom he is separated infinitely, is itself "the state of being grasped by the power of being-itself. . . . The power of this self-affirmation is the power of being which is effective in every act of courage. Faith is the experience of this power."[35]

If we read Tillich correctly, faith is the mirror that the courage to be holds up to itself. Should the analogy prove too static, we might alter it by saying that faith is a further expansion of the dynamism which is one with being's power, with being as being. Since faith accepts a God who transcends man infinitely and unconditionally, Faith accepts "in spite of"; and "out of the 'in spite of' of faith the 'in spite of' of courage is born."[36]

Rooting anxiety in man's confrontation with his own meontic non-being, Tillich sees the whole of the latter Middle Ages as a time when man was haunted by an overwhelming anxiety that constricted the human spirit. "The imagery of hell and purgatory drove people of the late Middle Ages to try various means of assuaging their anxiety: pilgrimages to holy places . . . ecclesiastical punishments and the desire for indulgences."[37] Death and guilt covered all Europe with their black imagery and the continent shuddered in its own fear of the Divine Wrath. Not itself the effect of doubt, medieval anxiety was the effect of the breakup of an older order of things that left man rootless and unsure of his own existence; but behind this particular form of anxiety lay the shudder before non-being which is the heart of all anxiety.

Tillich's reading of late medieval anxiety might seem arbitrary to some, and to others it might seem the fancy of a thinker who feels constrained to conceptualize the whole of reality exclusively in existentialist terms. But the substance of his judgments antedates the popularity of existentialism and can be found in historians and writers whose opinions owe nothing to Heideggerian terminology. There is a remarkable convergence here between the Protestant Paul Tillich, the secular humanist Thomas Mann, and the Catholic Hilaire Belloc.[38] All are agreed that the intensity of the Gothic spent itself within a scant three hundred years. Altogether lacking in that indolence and grace that we associate today with things Italian and Mediterranean, medieval man in full flood lived a life of vigor and religious passion that ended in exhaustion. The exhaustion was a mockery of what went before. Europe in decline—the Europe of gables and narrow streets, of snow and mean taverns, of the mockery of Villon and the tired treachery of Louis XI, of hired men in livery and heavy armor, of hoofs on cobbled streets—this Europe was filled with an unnatural passion for penance and a morbid preoccupation with death: German children on crusade in Italy; Paris filled with the *Danse Macabre*. It was a time when an uneasy fear of hell gripped the North and men who earlier would have stormed heaven now sought a ticket to purgatory. It was upon this, the winter of a heroic age, that the Reformation broke. It promised release from bondage, although it was defined by the very bondage that it attacked.[39] Man, according to the Protestant mind of Tillich, learned to accept God *in spite of* his own unworthiness:

The immense liberation brought to the people of the sixteenth century by the message of the Reformers and the creation of their indomitable courage to accept acceptance was due to the *sola fide* doctrine, namely to the message that the courage of confidence is conditioned not by anything finite but solely by that which is unconditional itself and which we experience as unconditional in a person-to-person encounter.[40]

Tillich captures the Reformation style of life in a passage that crystalizes the spare and restless world born in the sixteenth-century revolt against Rome. Tillich here is speaking of Luther's "courage of confidence," which is one with

Lutheran faith and which is a pure manifestation of the ontology of the power of being:

> It has been rightly said that Albrecht Dürer's engraving, "Knight, Death, and the Devil," is a classic expression of the spirit of the Lutheran Reformation and—it might be added—of Luther's courage of confidence, of his form of the courage to be. A knight in full armor is riding through a valley, accompanied by the figure of death on one side, the devil on the other. Fearlessly, concentrated, confident he looks ahead. He is alone but he is not lonely. In his solitude he participates in the power which gives him the courage to affirm himself in spite of the presence of the negativities of existence.[41]

It is evident not simply from Tillich's explicit statements, but from the whole temper of his work, that he thinks the Protestant affirmation of being as power, the Protestant experience of the "for Thine is the Power and the Glory forever," is not only one among the many authentic confrontations with existence that Tillich details for us in his *The Courage To Be*, but that it represents a supreme articulation by the human spirit of the very structure and meaning of being itself. Well aware that love has the primacy within Catholicism,[42] Tillich himself sees love as a function of self-affirmation, as an expression of the power of being in which being conquers alienation and unites itself with that from which being has been separated.[43] Doing justice to love as *philia*, as *eros*, and as agape (which latter is "love cutting into love . . . just as the Word of God is the Word cutting into all words,"[44] Tillich nonetheless sees the power structure of being as more fundamental, not in the sense that power opposes love (this happens only when love is without justice), but in the sense that love itself is ontologically meaningful only in terms of something more profound than itself, something of which love as such is a manifestation. This something, the Power of Being—expressed first in the Stoic insistence that man face evil and death with an indifference that steels him against the void; next breaking into the West with clarity in Spinoza's teaching that virtue and being are identical because virtue is a supreme actualization of nature and therefore its supreme affirmation or being, its conatus; experienced and articulated in full grandeur by Luther; born again in Nietzsche, who had "the courage to look into the abyss of nonbeing in the complete loneliness of him who accepts the message that 'God is dead' "[45]—is not only the very heart and meaning and center of human existence for Tillich, but is also man's finest symbol for the "God beyond the God of theism," the meaning which emerges even within the anguish of meaninglessness, the Ground of Being lying behind every human conception of the Divine.

Paul Tillich's system finds its depths and its limits in its ontology of God. Just as the ontology of power is deepened when seen in the light of the Protestant experience of faith, so too is the ontology of God deepened when seen in the light of the trinitarian formulas of Christianity. Tillich sees the specifically Christian doctrine of the Trinity as emerging out of Christology, but he insists that the trinitarian symbol is far older than Christianity[46] and is *demanded* when the philosophical mind takes seriously both the absoluteness and the concreteness of God. Although Tillich rejects any attempt to demonstrate the existence of the Holy

Trinity of Christian orthodoxy, we must remember that
both an analysis of ontological structures and their dialectical relations function within Tillich analogously to the way
in which demonstration functions within Aristotelianism.
Tillich's twentieth-century doctrine on the Trinity, facing
a secularized West with tools borrowed from existentialism
and from Hegelianism, reminds one of Blessed Raymond
Lull's fourteenth-century doctrine, facing the Moslems
with the instruments he inherited from Greek thought. But
whereas Blessed Raymond Lull saw the Holy Trinity as the
internal ecstasis of an infinite love and *therefore* implicated
within the structure of being as agape, Tillich sees trinitarian symbolization[47] of the ground of being as a dialectical
necessity rooted in the internal relations between being and
non-being; in short, Tillich sees a trinitarian symbolization
of the divine as a function of being as power. That both
Tillich and Lull have been accused (with or without justification is beyond the economy of this essay) by their respective coreligionists of reducing the data of Revelation to
philosophy strengthens the parallel. But although Tillich—
the Protestant—sees the trinitarian articulation of the divine
as a function of the power of being, Lull—the Catholic—
sees it as a "function" of the superabundant agape in which
being itself consists. The difference is not without interest
when related to Tillich's assertion that the power structure
of being as articulated in faith is characteristic of Protestantism and mystical love is characteristic of Catholicism. We
shall return to this issue again because it is the very nerve of
the whole argument of this book.

The doctrine of the Trinity is implicated in the dialectical movement of the real, insists Tillich. This dialectical

movement does not contradict the demands of formal logic wherein a Yes and a No, an affirmation and a negation, exclude one another, but is located in a deeper dimension of thought than is logic. Logic, we might say, is the structure of rational discourse, but dialectics are its dynamics. Within this movement affirmation and negation demand rather than exclude one another. Tillich's debt to Hegal in this point is explicitly mentioned by him.[48] Formal logic, therefore, is not contradicted when "the divine life is described as a trinity within a unity. The doctrine of the Trinity does not affirm the logical nonsense that three is one and one is three; it describes in dialectical terms the inner movement of the divine life as an eternal separation from itself and return to itself."[49] Tillich swiftly brushes away the somewhat naïve rationalist objection to the Trinity which cavils at the doctrine on the grounds that three cannot be one. "The answer to this question is given in every life process."[50]

Without non-being God would be an infinite abyss, chaos. "Nonbeing (that in God which makes his self-affirmation dynamic) opens up the divine self-exclusion and reveals him as power and love. Nonbeing makes God a living God. Without the No he has to overcome *in himself* and in his creature, the divine Yes to himself would be lifeless."[51] The infinite, therefore, embraces the finite in the sense that God's affirmation of His own Power to Be works through the whole of His creation and is the Ground of the power of being wherever it is encountered. God's assertion of Himself, His affirmation of the abyss of His own Divine Life, is the Logos, the Son, the form of God and therefore God as concrete. Tillich seems dissatisfied with the decision of Nicaea defended by St. Athanasius. Although Nicaea "saved Christianity from a relapse to a cult of half-gods,"[52] it left unanswered the question of "how a difference could exist between the Father and the Son."[53] In any event, the "idea of the 'living God' requires a distinction between the abysmal element of the divine, the form element, and their spiritual unity."[54] A god not subject to the law of the dialectic would be identified with the sterility of the concept of being as totally excluding non-being and as therefore undifferentiated; He would be the non-concrete-being that Hegel found in the concept of absolute being. God's internal differentiation involves His concretion and the return of that concretion to Himself in a higher unity involving both the absoluteness of the divine abyss and the meaningful expression of the Divine as Logos or internal revelation. God's self-affirmation and the assertion of His infinite Power over non-being *is* the Son as the very concrete Expression of the Father. The Spirit is their Unity.[55]

The Logos "opens up the divine ground, its infinity and its darkness, and it makes its fullness distinguishable, definite, *finite*."[56] Without the Logos God would be "demonic, characterized by absolute seclusion . . . the naked absolute of Luther." The problem of the finite character of the Logos as expression of the infinite power of being seems to be demanded by Tillich's dialectics of "concretion" but seems equally Arian as well. Tillich tries to escape trinitarian heresy by teaching that the Spirit

gives actuality to that which is potential in the divine ground and "outspoken" in the divine logos. Through the Spirit the divine fulness is posited in the divine life as something definite, and at the same time it is reunited in the divine ground. The finite is posited as finite within the process of the divine life, but is reunited with the infinite within the same process. It is distinguished from the infinite, but it is not separated from it.[57]

Reaffirming that his discussion of the trinitarian principles of the Divine "is not the Christian doctrine of the Trinity" but a "preparation for it, nothing more," Tillich insists nonetheless that the trinitarian principles "appear whenever one speaks meaningfully of the living God"[58] and that they are, therefore, one with the ontological structure of the Ground of Being, the power of being as such. Tillich's analysis of the trinitarian principle, as indicated throughout, is one with his analysis of the structure of being. As being must cross over into non-being by affirming itself against non-being, and thus by defining and structuring itself in proportion to this affirmation, so too God—the Ground of Being—is the Living God in that He affirms Himself in all His Infinity against the powers of darkness and absorbs within Himself the totality of non-being, me-ontic as well as ouk-ontic. This affirmation of God as the expression and form of His power, His Logos, corresponds analogically to the concretion which faith and the courage to be give to the power of being as ultimate structure of the real. Both point to Tillich's fundamental ontological position: this involves seeing being in its most radical meaning as involving a double negation, as that living center formed by the clash between being and non-being, two moments that can be separated from their clash only at the risk of removing them from reality and freezing them within the sterility of a logic that disguises itself as metaphysics.

Although some philosophers object strenuously to *any*

expression of their systems in psychological or literary terms, Tillich—owing to his use of the specifically psychological and to his insistence on the symbolic character of ontology—would not object, I trust, if I called his theory of being a "reality in the trenches" theory. Being here is dynamic, but the dynamism is one of defense and counterattack against the enemy. Using a phrase Tillich borrows from Luther and makes his own, we might say that for him being is not an *esse*, an "is" as in Aquinas; being is not an "as if," an *als ob* as in Vaihinger; being is rather a *trotz*, an "in spite of." But in truth is this the deepest meaning of being, to be an "in spite of"?

The Experience of Non-Being and the Western Tradition

WE HAVE seen that Tillich's dialectic of being and non-being involves their mutual interplay within existence. Existence, for the Protestant theologian, partakes of both being and non-being. Therefore Tillich rejects as spurious the question, Why is there something rather than nothing? At first sight it seems odd that Tillich, himself so heavily influenced by Heidegger, rules out of court that wonder before being which gives birth to a questioning about the very "why" of being itself. But possibly Tillich is wiser than his German master. If the question *why* something and not nothing is a valid question, then it follows that there is some factor within the real which prevents things from accounting for their existence. And if the mind judges that existence must be accounted for and that an existence unexplained would be absurd and irrational, then it follows that non-being does not enter into the structure of the real as a principle *demanded by being itself*. If this were the ontological situation, then we would have to ask why being *and not* non-being rather than why being *and* non-being, as asks Tillich. If being *as being* does not demand non-being, then the threat of non-being which surrounds us must be located within some principle which is not implicated within being *as being*. Given this latter possibility as true, we would have to conclude that it would be absurd to seek the reason for non-being within being. We would have to reject Tillich's power of being as the deepest meaning within reality.

Tillich's position involves the following reasoning: if being is the power to be, then being must be defined in terms of that against which this power of being is exercised, in terms of that against which being affirms itself, namely, non-being. A recognition of the validity of the question *why* being and not non-being would force Tillich into one of two positions unacceptable to him. He would have to accept a metaphysics which finds the intelligibility of finite being in its Cause, God. This would involve Tillich's accepting some rational demonstration for the existence of God. Rather than do this he prefers the paradox of a system that holds both the ontological necessity of the trinitarian principle *and* the impossibility of demonstrating the existence of the One God. The only alternative to rational demonstration is an irrationalism that would admit the question, Why being? but deny any answer because the universe is fundamentally absurd. The first possibility would lead Tillich toward Thomism and the second toward Sartreanism. The Protestant theologian declines both gambits.

Tillich is right, of course, in insisting that the "shock of non-being" lies very near if not at the heart of all genuine philosophizing, but this shock can take on different forms which heighten or obscure the hideousness of the nothing. Tillich himself speaks of differing kinds of anxiety arising from differing ways in which man experiences non-being. The philosphical articulation of the nothing or of non-being will always take its departure from the concrete historical soil in which man experiences anxiety. The validity of any of these articulations must be tested by fully philosophical criteria; nonetheless these philosophical efforts to penetrate the nothing depend on the *kind* of nothing encountered (if I may be permitted the phrase). It follows that an understanding of the experience is intrinsic to its philosophical penetration. Experiences are quite obviously neither valid nor invalid; they are just themselves. Philosophical authenticity depends on what we do with them. This is eminently true of Western man's confrontation with the nothing. The medieval Christian awareness of non-being was of sin and the lack of necessity within creation. The former produced anxiety before the God of justice and the latter humility before the Giver of being. The contemporary existentialist encounter with non-being is the experience of a supposed nothingness after death, of annihilation. In any event, the experience of the powers of non-being are one with what

Xavier Zubiri calls the "horizon" within which philosophy takes its point of departure.[59]

Other forms of contemporary anxiety emerge from this shock before total meaninglessness and absurdity. The very cracking of outer space by modern man has heightened this confrontation with an absolute of affirmation or negation. No one can fail to see, wrote Whittaker Chambers after the launching of the first Russian satellite, "that closing time is a distinct possibility."[60] Today nature is neither the jungle of the Yucatan nor is it the domesticated vineyards of the Mediterranean. Nature is that complex of power and terror that yesterday exploded over Hiroshima and that today spat a new moon into space. Nature has now been taken into the heart of human history and the very existence of the cosmos is from this day joined to the destiny of the human race. Henceforth existence itself shall be implicated in the counsels of human freedom. We have reached the final crisis: being or non-being. We have confronted the frontiers of meaning because we have faced the nothing that lies beyond being. Auden was right, insists Tillich, in calling ours "The Age of Anxiety." The very chaos of modern art as well as the advent of existential analysis attests the rare heroism needed to confront nakedly and without illusions the absurdity of a humanity wheeling all the resources of the spirit into battle array in order the better to fight—Nothing! Existence becomes more problematic the more it is swept into the terrible freedom of a creature posed between heaven and hell. In the past when a man questioned being, he questioned himself because he was a being; but in the future when a man questions himself, he will question the whole of being.

It is within this historical context that Tillich confronts being and non-being. Without categorizing Tillich's ontology as provincial (in a sense *all* ontologies are provincial), we are justified in seeing in it an articulation which grows out of a unique way in which man confronts anxiety and non-being. A comparison of the contemporary confrontation with meaninglessness with those found in other typical moments within Western history may not merely enable us to locate Tillich the better within the history of philosophy, but it might also reveal theoretical weaknesses within his position that are one with the necessarily limited experience from out of which his ontology was born.

Following Zubiri, I would say that the horizon within which a philosophy comes to birth is not something simply negative. We are not concerned necessarily with an "end situation" in which man finds himself shipwrecked, in Karl Jaspers' sense of the term. The cultural horizon not only limits but also defines and therefore makes possible philosophical discourse. All answers depend on the questions we ask and reality can speak to us only in terms of the language we use. These questions antedate any metaphysical system and emerge as a result of the way in which a civilization experiences reality. Zubiri insists that this experience need not be, and in fact usually is not, some supremely personal intuition. It is rather a corporate reaction to reality expressed in art, preserved in law, perpetuated in song. It is a response to the ultimate written on the tablets of history. Any philosophical understanding requires an imaginative and highly disciplined penetration into the cultural horizon within which philosophy comes to life.

The Greek horizon encompassed a world whose boundaries were defined by the heavens above and whose center was man. As I have written in another place,

the men of classical antiquity . . . had a well-defined place in the universe. They took their stance at the centre of an earth that was the centre of a universe composed of nine concentric spheres that turned cyclically in a movement that forever returned upon itself. Classical man, sailing across the Adriatic on a star-filled night, looked up and saw a sky that was literally the vault of heaven. The world existed for the ancients exactly as they took it into their eyes. Man was at home in this world because it was limited as is man himself. It was a world proportioned to a finite intellect and a finite sensibility. Beyond it there was nothing.[61]

Within this sharply defined universe a hierarchy of forms guaranteed and composed the order of the cosmos. Whether the forms stood behind the commerce of existence as in Plato or whether they were intrinsic to it as in Aristotle, they were always conceived as constituting the stability and the ontological consistency of reality. The Greek discovery of the logos was the Greek discovery of the faculty of the immutable, the eye of reality. The power of the logos to marshal all things before man, and then seize upon that within them which constituted their identity and their immutable structure, was a revelation to the Hellenic spirit of the true fatherland of the intelligence. The mind lives in the land of the "always."[62] "Philosophers only are able to grasp the eternal and unchangeable, and those who wander in the region of the many and variable are not philosophers."[63]

The Greek discovery of *nature* extended beyond the

physical cosmos to include the human world within an order of laws whose changelessness governed human conduct and political existence itself. Classical man was content to live within a harmonious universe whose very harmony Plato likened to a divine music. Being was a symphony orchestrated from within by musicians who played not by ear but by sheets of music that were as old and as young as was the eternal composition of the world.

The enemy of the harmony of reality for the Greek mind was change, movement of all kinds. Ortega, as we have seen, pointed out that Greek philosophizing about being occurred within the context of movement, and it was only the supreme genius of Aristotle, himself a product of the very extremity of the Greek world and a late flower within Greek culture, that succeeded in some measure in domesticating mobility by marshaling it under the laws of act and potency. Before Aristotle change is something that oppresses the Hellenic spirit. Parmenides tries to drive it away from a mind that would not have its dream of harmony and order disturbed by the nightmare of chaos. Plato freezes change into the form of the Other and thus disguises its disrupting power by fitting it into his ontological mosaic. Guardini has written of "the power of dissolution and corruption" that "so deeply oppressed the man of Greece."[64] Zubiri reminds us that it was not nothingness but corruption and age that clogged the Hellenic spirit as the supreme enemies of the order and harmony of being.

The Hellenic solution was a compromise. The individual is born to grow old and die, but the species remains. One polity degenerates and is replaced by another, but the cycle of existence guarantees the return of the prototype. The individual must hide his idiosyncrasies (rooted as they are in the darkness of matter) behind the decent anonymity of the mask, the *persona*, which represents the type and therefore the universal and perpetually valid meaning of the human comedy. Real being is changeless, but change and individuality are conditions for existence. Nothing significantly new can happen because a universe which is finite in structure and infinite in time has already opened every door; but that the same old doors be opened at all is the result of the youth and age, the generation and corruption of the things and men that are.

Paul Tillich teaches us that all anxiety is rooted in non-being, and that anxiety differs from fear in that fear confronts a concrete object, whereas anxiety is a state of dread lacking any specific enemy.[65] The doctrine, Kierkegaardian in origin, is now commonly accepted in contemporary European philosophy and psychology. What is significant about the distinction for our purposes here is the fact that forms of anxiety reveal the ways in which man confronts the nothing. The Greek world horizon confronted non-being primarily as the enemy to *order*. The chaotic and demonic forces of death and corruption and rebellion menace the very hierarchy of being, and the only release from anxiety was a return to order, most specifically to that divine and human order in which man found himself located through the very fact of his existence.

Today we are fortunate in having at hand for the first time in history a theoretical articulation of the problem of order. I refer to Eric Voegelin's monumental *Order and History*.[66] Man's experience of order, teaches Voegelin, is located within the structure of participation. Man is not "something" that can pick up and lay down at will his own participation in being. "Man" does not stand beyond the "being" of which he participates. He is rather that mysterious reality within being which is capable of experiencing itself as such and which is capable of the act of evocation. Man is, so to speak, the tongue of being. But the full articulation of his being would entail the articulation of the whole of which man participates as a part. The fact that this is impossible, often crushing to the human spirit, is the beginning and the end of human wisdom. Within this darkness which is the mystery of man shines whatever light can be found this side of paradise.

Voegelin maintains that three massive experiences dominate man's hunt for the meaning of his own existence. The first of these is marked by the dominance of the sense of participation. Grasping himself so completely one with the moving panorama of being that the gods become the fields and the valleys, man merges himself with the universe. Here man's participation in being is so accentuated that it tends to destroy itself and become a primitive, magical identity blocking effective rational action in the world. The second typical feature is a preoccupation with the truth that things come into and go out of existence but that existence itself remains. Lasting and passing are partners in the community of being. Each thing and each man dies, but being itself endures. From this fundamental experience arises the awareness of mortality and the symbol of immortality. The exploration of death as though it were a thing in itself reveals nothing more than "the nothing which makes us shudder with anxiety from the bottom of existence." And this anxiety passes beyond the fear of biological death and corruption and reaches to the horror of "losing, with the passing of existence, the slender foothold in the partnership of being that we experience as ours while existence lasts." The third experience is man's attempt to create symbols which reflect his experience of the unknown and known aspects of being.

Within the Greek world, insists Voegelin, the myths surrounding early Hellenic history point toward the Greek symbolization of the human soul as the eye of reality and the mirror of the order of being. The anxiety of Achilles, his "wrath," points to a gap in the order of being that binds mankind into a partnership with the laws of nature and her gods.[67] Homer confronts Achilles with the certain knowledge that he will die in battle and gain an imperishable fame if he will but remain in Troy and fight it out with the enemy. But if Achilles goes home the campaign will end ingloriously. Achilles, however, will return to the ease and repose of a princely life. The alternatives facing Achilles are banal and as fiction the tale has less interest than most romantic novels of the last century. But as myth the tale is something else. Its extraordinary power is centered in the fact that death has become an actuality for Achilles and not merely a remote possibility. Isolated from the common life of the camp, from the duties and decencies of human life by his obsession with death, Achilles becomes a type of mankind as such. War and hardship and danger and ultimate death are not merely risks attendant upon man's obligation to restore public order, but they are the "fated essence of human existence." The surrender to anxiety not only drains Achilles of heroism, but it strips him of humanity. His horror before the certainty of death paralyzes his power to live. Confronted with his fate as a soldier, with his destiny as a human being, Achilles sulks in his tent and the morale of the troops outside is shaken by the cowardly wrath of their leader. When we rage against the inevitable tragedy of life, human order is corrupted and the death we would escape in the battlefield of life now haunts the rear echelons of the human spirit. Where there was order there is now chaos; where there was harmony, now dissonance; where there was peace within war, now there is war within the mockery of peace. As Voegelin puts it so eloquently,

This outburst [of Achilles against his fate] rightly causes uneasiness in the others because it is sensed as an absolute threat to the meaning of order. For the game of order, with its partial diminutions and restitutions, can be played only as long as life is accepted with a will to act it out regardless of the mystery of death. If death is not accepted as a mystery in life, as part of the mystery of life itself, if the attempt is made to transform the mystery through reflection into an experience of something, of a reality, then the reality of death will become the nothingness which destroys the reality of life. When a walking ghost like Achilles appears on the scene, the pallor of death falls over the game of order; it can no longer be taken seriously and the drama sputters out in futility and disorder.[68]

Homer's resolution of the dilemma, says Voegelin, begins with the Trojan attack which penetrates the Greek camp. Achilles, at first quite willing to let his comrades perish, is shocked back into life by the death of his friend, Patroclus (*Iliad*, XVIII, 78–126). He is awakened by his awareness that not only he but all men die. He returns to his life within the community resolutely determined to shoulder his obligations, even to the extremity of death. Death loses its horror when life again has become so supremely real that it is not worth living except on its own conditions. Achilles kills Hector in battle and then accepts his fate.

The myth has enormous consequences for the theory of non-being. In the first place, the myth shows us that non-being cannot be understood as such. We must say that the absolute exclusion of being from non-being makes of non-being the final cross upon which the human spirit will crucify itself inexorably should man try to cross the frontier of being. Non-being simply cannot be articulated intellectually or experienced imaginatively without turning it into something which is not itself, into some fancied or effective being whose contemplation is the very agent of chaos and the herald of the destruction of human personality. The way in which an individual or a society articulates its own anxiety before non-being will be determined by that society's lived experience of being. We have seen that being for the Hellenic mind is structure, form, self-consistency, identity, in a word—order. As Achilles turns away from non-being as the enemy of divine and human order, so too does the Greek philosophical mind see the non-being of change and corruption as the falling away from a previously given unity and order. Even when unity and excellence demand change, the change is left behind when being in full actuality achieves that Eleatic consistency and stability in which being was thought to consist. An even further domestication of non-being was attempted by Plato and it remains among the permanent monuments to the Hellenic salute to the immutable. In Plato the logic of negation urges him to reduce the reality of the form of non-being to the form of the other. If the judgment "Socrates is not flying" means anything at all, then "not flying" is a real form inhering in Socrates constituting him in his otherness. Non-being here does not act as a limit upon being but is admitted within being and takes its place with all other forms and ideas. In the words of Antonio Millan Puelles, "Non-being here is not that which is deprived of form, but it is the very form of deprivation itself: *El no ser es aquí, no la falta de forma, sino la forma del faltar.*"[69] Here the hound of non-being is made to ride with the pack of forms that make up reality. One can scarcely conceive of a more complete victory for the Hellenic powers of order over the forces of chaos.

But the myth reveals something still more profound than the psychological and intellectual impossibility of confronting the nothing face to face. Achilles returns to the world and assumes his responsibilities, both to his own personal destiny and to his fellow soldiers, by affirming himself against his own "wrath," by conquering his anxiety before the nothingness of his fate. Here we have an almost classical instance of what Paul Tillich means by the courage to be. If order is a form of being and if chaos is a form of non-being, then certainly their relations reveal the power of being over non-being. But Homer introduces a third element which makes us pause before accepting uncritically Professor Tillich's dialectic. Achilles comes alive to his responsibilities as a result of the death of his friend, Patroclus. It is the love that the reserved and removed figure of Achilles had for his companion that galvanizes him

into the action which culminates in the death of Hector
and in his own.

Why does Achilles face his destiny? The answer is not
far to seek. Love moved Achilles to affirm himself. Love
primed the courage to be. It is the newborn love that
Achilles feels for his companions, a love stirred in the ashes
of his own desolation and bitterness over the death of a
friend—a man he had cherished and who is now dead—
that moves Achilles to take up the sword once again. If
the myth reveals anything at all, it most certainly reveals
that the courage to be is itself born of a love that transcends the tragedy of fate.

For Tillich, love is the union of the separated achieved
by the power of self-affirmation; this affirmation englobes
the other and therefore heals alienation. This is a delicate
analysis of what love *does*, but it leaves unanswered what
love *is* and therefore is concerned with the result, not the
cause. Love moves Achilles to assert his being, the being of
a soldier, a prince, and a leader of men; but this new
courage was a consequence of love and not its cause. It is
certainly a matter of common experience that moral courage and physical courage are often born in a coward precisely at the moment when those he loves deeply are
menaced. The affirmation of his being in a courage that
conquers his fears and anxiety is prodded into being by
his love. Because he loves, he is brave and often brave even
unto death. The dialectic between being and non-being is
more complicated than Tillich makes it out to be.

Greek anxiety before non-being is conquered, therefore,
by the Greek love of order in all its forms, and Greek
anxiety is rooted in the confrontation with non-being that

underlies all anxiety. In the Hellenic world this anxiety takes the form of a reaction against disorder and chaos. The Greeks never questioned being as such and therefore did not ask themselves the question that Tillich maintains is unaskable: Why is there being at all and why not non-being? This question made sense only within the Catholic, Christian world that had known the meaning of creation as the free gift of a God whose name was Being. Within the context of the Christian world, both patristic and medieval, being takes on a radically contingent character. The universe exists, but absolutely speaking it does not have to exist. The horizon within which man philosophized was more than broadened. We might justly speak here of a "crack through" of the human spirit to the very problematic structure of existence as such. Contingency within the classical world looks back to an event which need not have been and forward to an event which need not be. Whatever could be traced to the necessity of law obeyed the ordered structure of reality, but whatever could not be so traced, be it past or future, was laid to the door of chance and fate, themselves the enemies of a classical order that eventually failed because it could make no sense out of the victory of the chaos of barbarism.[70] But contingency within the Christian world extended to the very *being* of the universe as such. Here contingency does not mean "need not *have been*" but "need not *be*." But if the universe of being need not be, then why is it at all? The Christian answer to this question seems deceptively simple to us only because we still live within a world whose horizons were created by the Faith. The universe of being *is* simply because God caused it to be. Why did God cause it? Because He willed to. Why did He so will? The question admits of no answer because it is lost in the mystery of Divine Freedom. Rephrasing the issue, we can say that the answer to this question is not a "reason" but something transcending all reasons: love. There is being rather than nothing because there is love. Love is not a reason, but it is a cause. What love does to the beloved is precisely that: that is, it makes him *be*-loved which in turn can make or break his life, depending on what he does with the gift, as all poetry proclaims and all life declaims. But the issue is more radical when it touches the roots of being as such. What being-*loved* makes being do is precisely *be*. Here love does not come to being as does a gift to one who receives the gift. In the words of Gerald Smith, "if creation be a gift, it is not a gift made to us; we are the gift."[71]

It follows that the primacy of love within being forced Catholic Christianity to look at being in terms of its contingency, in terms of its not having to be. The experience of non-being within this cultural horizon is one with the experience of the gratuity of Divine Love. This experience of the primacy of love within being altogether crossed the great medieval debate between voluntarists and intellectualists. Both were in absolute agreement about the gratuity of creation and the radical contingency of finite being. As a consequence, the metaphysically ultimate explanation for the universe of finite being is the love of God rather than His power. He has the power, undoubtedly, to have created another order of things, but the fact that He created this one can be traced to the mystery of His freedom, to His love.

When the issue is shifted to the properly ontological

structure of finite being as we confront it, we are forced to ask the question we raised before. If no given being has to be, where do we seek this intrinsic non-necessity of its being? Philosophers asked the question because the Christian vision of being as created prompted them to ask it. But the philosophical answer to the question involves our finding some factor within the real which prevents things accounting for their own being. Non-being, however, cannot enter the structure of the real as demanded by being itself if the question why being and not non-being is a valid question. It follows that the threat of non-being, the root of the nothingness menacing all things, must be located within being itself but not identified with the principle or principles accounting for being as such. The strategy is densely metaphysical and highly paradoxical because it pretends to find within being something accounting for the possibility of non-being, which "something," however, actually is being but is not the principle of being.

St. Thomas Aquinas' answer to the question was couched in terms of his famous distinction between "to be" and essence or nature. It would be superfluous here to repeat what has been amply documented by a vast literature concerning this celebrated distinction. Suffice it to say that the strategy motivating Aquinas' metaphysics was laid down early in his career in his *De Ente et Essentia*. Some Thomists, such as Hawkins, think the *De Ente* is heavily under the influence of Avicenna.[72] Others see in it an early map of the entire thought of St. Thomas.[73] A contemporary Spanish philosopher, Pedro Caba, has suggested recently that the analysis within the *De Ente et Essentia* yields a dynamic notion of being which St. Thomas failed to exploit.[74] It is probable that all three judgments are true and reconcilable. Before elaborating his metaphysics of being as act of existing, Aquinas had to isolate being from essence or nature. Avicenna and Al-Farabi had already groped toward such an isolation. Only after having determined the metaphysical "otherness" of existence to essence could Aquinas elaborate a metaphysics of existence as act; but in the course of isolating this radical principle of being St. Thomas uncovered the roots of contingency and non-being. He found them within the very composed structure of the real as we encounter it within our experience.

In the *De Ente et Essentia*, St. Thomas teaches that the being of any nature cannot be reduced to that nature itself, and that it does not flow forth from that nature.[75] The formal and material principles composing any existing substance have no being in themselves, cannot exist in isolation from the substance, and therefore cannot *be* the substance in its existentiality. The fact that one and the same nature can be in more than one being and in more than one order of being eliminates any Greek reduction of being to nature or formality. Secondly, a nature generating its own being would already have to be prior to this act of generating and this would involve its being before it was. Thus being is not a function or property of nature. St. Thomas draws two conclusions from this reasoning: (a) being is other than nature; (b) nature is dependent on its own being because without that being nature is simply nothing.[76] Two statements can be made, therefore, about the being or *esse* of any limited thing. First, *esse* or being is related to essence and this relation is non-necessary, contingent. Being is prior to its receptive subject. But being is prior in such a way as not to be a thing in itself or to have the essence as *its* property or possession. (For this reason we cannot speak of the "essence of an existence," although we can of the "essence of an existent.") Were the essence of a tree the property of the being of the tree, then the tree would not be but rather the being of the tree! This flatly contradicts the evidence. It is *things* themselves, *substances*, which are beings. Essence, although posterior to its own being or *esse*, is necessarily the subject of its own being.

If this reasoning seems bewildering at first sight, it is because the *esse* of St. Thomas is an oddity when expressed in terms proper to the metaphysics of Aristotle. Here we have an ontological principle—the principle of all principles—which is "accidental" to essence only in the sense that it forms no part of essence and in the sense that essence cannot lay claim to being simply by presenting its credentials as essence. But although "accidental" to essence in this broadened sense of the word, essence is purely and simply nothing without existence.[77] A double dependence emerges here which makes absolutely necessary the question, Why something rather than nothing? Aristotle had already taught Aquinas, and continues to teach us, that whatever is not being in itself must be being through something else and therefore must be dependent upon that through which it is being. This truth is an induction from the facts of experience. The substantial nature is dependent on its very being or *esse;* cancel the being of the substance, and the substance has been cancelled. But the being of the substance, the *esse* of the substance, as a consequence of *its* own failure to be in itself (that is, existence does not exist), as a result of functioning as the very *be*-ing of the substance, is itself dependent. This principle of existence cannot be dependent on the substantial nature which depends upon it. "To be" can only be dependent upon something which is capable of causing it. Ultimately, of course, Aquinas reasons to the existence of the Pure Act of Being as sole cause of the being of all dependent natures.

What is important for us here within the economy of this study is the ambiguous status of essence or nature. Always encountered as being and known to be encounterable only as being, essence is other than its own being. Although a subsequent and more refined metaphysical analysis reveals nature to be the intrinsic limit upon being, the analysis within the *De Ente et Essentia* reveals being as that which is received by nature from beyond nature's own capacities, capacities which are in fact posited only by *esse* itself. Were nature an absolute non-being (ouk-ontic non-being), nature could never be. Actually, nature is a kind of me-ontic non-being but not simply in the way in which Paul Tillich understands me-ontic non-being. For Tillich, me-ontic non-being is that out of which I have emerged and which I am no longer, and that present nothingness of myself which I will actualize at some future point within my life. The first is Ortega's the "has been" of the past, the being I have left behind me on my march through life. The second is Zubiri's "field of possibilities" which makes the future realizable. But me-ontic non-being in St. Thomas is something still more radical: it is the *here and now* not-having-to-be of that which is. Contingency and necessity meet in a paradox written into the structure of being. It is necessary that a being *be* so long as it is, but *the being* which is, even while it is, need not be because there is nothing within its essence demanding that it be. The paradox can be worded as follows, I would suggest: *Whereas nature is always implicated within being, being is never implicated within nature*. In the words of Joseph Owens,

natures "contribute to their being a deficiency, its limitation. . . . of their own nature (beings) have no being
whatsoever, either in the intellect or in reality."[78]

Medieval philosophy in general and the philosophy of
St. Thomas in particular have been accused of reducing
non-being to the logical negation found in judgment and
therefore of draining human life of its tragic dimension.
Nothing could be less true. The mystery of *non-being is*
one with the participated structure of finite reality. Only
in God is being a nature in the sense of being a "what." In
all other things being is participated. Nature here means not
only "what" a being is but the "limit" upon being. The universe is truly a universe of beings and from this point of
view non-being has no positive ontological status. But the
universe of being is being solely by participation. It follows
that *by nature the universe of things is nothing at all.* Re-
move the being the universe received from God and the
universe itself has been removed. In a sense the question is
not why being rather than nothing, but why are all these
ontological "nothings" by nature doing an act of being?
Why are they when *of themselves* they are so many zeros?

Here the dialectic between being and non-being is something different from what we found in Professor Tillich.
For Tillich the religious symbol of "the Fall" answers an
ontology in which man falls from essential into existential
being. Sin, therefore, is the theological symbol for the
dialectic between being and non-being and sin is written
into the heart of existence as such. (Let us remember that
"existence" for Tillich does not mean simply being; it
means "standing in" and "standing out" of being.) But
within the Catholic metaphysics of Aquinas the Fall can
never be from essence into existence; existence, here looked

upon as the highest act and the source of all perfection limited from within by essence, is not a state into which one "falls." Estrangement and guilt and alienation are made possible by the essential multiplicity in which man is created, and the root of the Fall must be found within man's essence, not within his existence. The Church finds it within his will. The Council of Trent says that only grace can conquer. An awareness of the nothingness we are by nature can awaken in us a prayer of thanksgiving for the gift of being and a prayer of hope that the Providence through which we are will watch over us and lead us into the fatherland. The shock of non-being can stir within the mind a questioning as to why we are at all when every resource within our very nature cries out its own radical insufficiency and ontological poverty. When thus shaken to the foundation, the only alternative to anxiety is gratitude. This gratitude in truth is a grace, the kind of grace the Church calls "actual," which can be any person or thing that lights up the night in which we live. But when gratitude is so profound that it reaches within to my very being and beyond to the whole of being to which I am related, then gratitude answers Love. This is a mystery because the answer to Love is love itself.

The Primacy of Love Within the Catholic Order

WE ARE indebted to Professor Tillich for pointing out the truth that ontological systems cannot be built around end situations, although they can be tested by them. Tillich ex-

ploits, in the name of Protestant courage, the end situation
of the courage to be before the final despair in which man's
power to assert himself against the terrors of the darkness
reveal a meaning within meaninglessness, a God who appears when "the God of theism has disappeared in the
anxiety of doubt." I suggest that when man confronts suicide as a real possibility he there finds tested in fire his sense
of allegiance to being and to himself. The way in which the
Catholic tradition has met the suicide is illustrative of the
primacy which that tradition has given love over power
as a final meaning within being itself.

Suicide within Catholic civilization has almost always
been the effect of madness, sudden or come to maturity
slowly. The pagan world justified suicide and the Far
Eastern world gives us examples of men who kill themselves with their eyes open, fully conscious of what they
do. I would be the last to deny a heroism and even nobility
to these traditions, especially to the Japanese, but the very
possibility of an ethic permitting suicide has always been
rejected energetically and almost fanatically by Catholic
civilization. No one has stated this position better than
G. K. Chesterton in his *Orthodoxy:*

Not only is suicide a sin, it is the sin. It is the ultimate and absolute evil, the refusal to take an interest in existence; the refusal to take the oath of loyalty to life. . . . A martyr is a man
who cares so much for something outside him, that he forgets
his own personal life. A suicide is a man who cares so little for
anything outside him, that he wants to see the last of everything. One wants something to begin: the other wants everything to end. . . . The suicide is ignoble because he has not this
link with being: he is a mere destroyer; spiritually, he destroys

the universe. And then I remembered the stake and the cross-
roads, and the queer fact that Christianity had shown this weird
harshness to the suicide. For Christianity had shown a wild
encouragement to the martyr. Historic Christianity was accused, not entirely without reason, of carrying martyrdom and
asceticism to a point, desolate and pessimistic. The early Christian martyrs talked of death with a horrible happiness. They
blasphemed the beautiful duties of the body; they smelt the
grave afar off like a field of flowers. All this has seemed to
many the very poetry of pessimism. Yet there is the stake at
the cross-roads to show what Christianity thought of the pessi-
mist.[79]

If we turn to St. Thomas Aquinas on the same subject,
we find a parallel confirmation of Chesterton's position in
one of the most curious and profound articles in the *Summa
Theologiae*.[80] I say the article is curious because Aquinas,
addressing himself to the problem of suicide, does not pro-
ceed as we might imagine he would. He does not begin as
would a moralist by pointing to the truth that God, the
Author of life, alone has the right to take it away. This
argument is but the third advanced in the body of the article
and it is subordinate to the first two arguments, which are
metaphysical rather than juridical or ethical in character.
Those who accuse St. Thomas of an excessively legalistic
ethics ought to ponder carefully this passage because here
Aquinas roots the ethical squarely within the ontological.

Each being, begins St. Thomas, loves itself naturally. Because it loves itself naturally, each being resists corruption
and death to the degree lying within its power. To kill oneself is an act against the very inclination of nature, and, adds
St. Thomas pointedly, it is a sin against charity because each

being ought to love itself. The key phrases are *naturaliter quaelibet res seipsum amat* (each thing loves itself naturally); and *conservat se in esse et corrumpentibus resistit quantum potest* (each thing conserves itself in being and resists corruption to the degree to which it can). The love which a being has of itself is natural. By this word "natural" St. Thomas does not mean nature in the strict sense of essence. It is axiomatic that Aquinas holds all love to be a response to the good, and things are good only when they exist and to the extent to which they exist. For this reason St. Thomas often denies that abstractions such as mathematical concepts are good. They lack being and therefore cannot be loved. We can only love to know them because our knowing them is itself being and is therefore lovable. The "natural" love a being has for itself is neither an essential determination of being nor is it an addition to being. Being is desirable in simple being, is lovable in the very exercise of the act of existence. This assertion is too primitive to be demonstrated, but it can be tested by a reduction to the absurd: that is, by a reduction to nothingness because only the nothing is absurd. Could being love or desire its opposite, non-being? But non-being is nothing and nothing cannot be loved; better yet, an act of loving nothing would be a non-act, itself nothing, because an act of love is structured by its term. Hatred of being lies on the side of negation and non-being. The profound neurotic guilt that rots away the sanity of so many people in our day is itself rooted in a hatred for the very being of the self, a hatred which breeds a carelessness before being that often issues into derangement and suicide. By locating love in the very heart of being, Aquinas fingers the source whence flow all conscious desire and election, which are themselves nothing more than elicited confirmations of the radical goodness of existence. The love of which we speak is a love which is the ground of all love, be it the love of agape or the love of *eros*. From this it follows, maintains the Angelic Doctor, that "being conserves itself in being and resists corruption to the extent to which it can": *potest!*

This is Professor Tillich's "power of being," his "courage to be." The power of being is being's ratification of its own goodness, its own desirability. This is an affirmation behind all conscious affirmation. It is being's saying "let it be" to itself because "it is good that being be." Hence no being dissolves itself voluntarily, no being gives up existence without a fight. No being consents passively to its own nothingness. This truth extends beyond the order of individual beings to the very *order* of being as such; it englobes the social and makes intelligible political and cultural resistance to alteration and to change. Politically, it was articulated, with a compactness impossible to match, by Abraham Lincoln's "No state voluntarily consents to its own destruction." If the ecstatic structure of being bespeaks generosity and superabundance, then there follows from it necessarily what might be called its corelative, the conservative principle of being: this is Professor Tillich's the power to be and it is St. Thomas' "each thing *conserves* itself in being . . . to the extent to which it can." Divided often on the conscious level of decision, where the freedom of man is capable of disturbing the equilibrium of the harmony of existence, the ecstatic and the conservative or *resistant* in being are one and the same paradox, a paradox that forms existence as such.

The power of being against the forces of corruption and nothingness is a function of being's love of itself. The ground of this power is love, says St. Thomas. Here is a sword cleaving asunder the Protestant world of Tillich and the Catholic world of Aquinas. The question here does not look to who is right on the issue: both are right and each admits the insights of the other. The question looks to the supremacy of love or power, of the ecstatic or the tragic. For the Protestant world, as interpreted by Tillich, being's power to be is the condition of love, which in turn is being's affirmation of the other, the beloved. For Tillich, love is being's assertion of itself and of its right to be united to the other. Love thus follows on power, on the courage to be. When being is thus experienced, as it has been within the Protestant world, the tragic dimensions of existence take precedence over the ecstatic. Protestantism has had good reason to conclude the Lord's Prayer with the splendid "For Thine is the Power and the Glory." The Power and the Glory: this is the Protestant God, ground of all power, Power Itself, the Glory of Being. Tillich is not duped by the meaning of modern industrialism; he sees clearly that the immense revolution achieved in Protestant countries during the modern era has had nothing to do essentially with the practical problems of "raising the standard of living." The new revolution has been modern man's affirmation of being, his power against the negativities of life. The enormous commercial and mercantile stirring that marked the whole Calvinist world of the seventeenth century was a form of the Protestant power to be, a declaration of the worth of personal existence against the void. The essentially resistant and even conservative character of the English

Revolution against the Stuarts was born in men who wrestled day and night with the Lord, who achieved a dignity and a right to be by insisting on parliamentary government against the prerogative of the Crown. The world that issued from the Calvinist Revolution was stern and unlovely. It was unmarked by the grace of the old order it supplanted. But it was a world that met a need—the need of free men to assert their own freedom and test it in the fire of battle, the need of free men to affirm the value of their own existence. If the philosophical foundations of modern democracy are more medieval than modern, we must nonetheless admit with all candor that the psychological and *ontological* foundations are thoroughly Protestant. No man with any insight into the history of the Anglo-Saxon world could justly say otherwise.

Within the Catholic world the ecstatic dominates the tragic because being's power to be against negation, being's courage and fortitude, are experienced as flowing out of a natural superabundance within being itself. The response to being within Catholic culture is lavish, uneconomic, in a word—chivalric. This is the deepest secret of the Baroque, a world thrown into existence as a gauntlet of defiance lifted against the bourgeois and Calvinist North. Were we to contrast the two worlds face to face on the field of battle, we might well remember Naseby where Oliver Cromwell, moved to prayer by the sight of the gaily colored and brilliantly bannered Royalist army drawn up against him and his somberly clad, psalm-singing Ironsides, wrote "that God would, by things that are not, bring to naught things that are." It would be difficult to match for terseness this expression of the Protestant courage before negation. That same morning in the opposite lines a Catholic Cavalier wrote his sweetheart that "this day I shall strike a great blow for my gracious Lord, the King." Here is the spirit of Crashaw and Lovelace and of all the Cavalier poets, the spirit of St. Paul's and of Van Dyke, the ecstasy of Bernini. These decisions for the tragic and for the ecstatic, articulated consciously in philosophical systems and political decisions, are themselves initially responses to a reality whose springs are profoundly and often obscurely theological.

If we return to the text of St. Thomas, we note that his second argument against suicide fingers the relation between "natural" love and ecstatic love, a relation left obscure in his first argument. Whatever is part of a whole belongs to that whole and is, analogically, the whole itself. Aquinas cites Aristotle and refers specifically to the political community of which the person is a member; but what he says of the political community can be extended to the *comunitas entis*—to the total community of finite being. As part of the community, the suicide injures the whole in killing himself. In effect he wills the death of all creation, according to the text cited from Chesterton. Suicide leaves a wound in being, a fissure which can never be filled because no man can ever play the role of another within the economy of existence. In loving myself I love the whole of being of which I am a part. And in loving the whole I love myself. Here the opposition between agape and *eros* is transcended because of the very structure of participation and intentionality. Man not only both is and is not the whole of which he participates—being—but man only participates in being by opening himself to reality in its wholeness. His loyalty to the world is his loyalty to himself. On this level of ontological penetration, it is impossible to distinguish between agape and *eros,* or, more accurately, it is possible to finger their union and their common source.

Expressing the issue in terms of intentionality and therefore elevating it to the properly human, we can say that man's love of himself is his love of the other *because* his love of himself is his own being. *An act whose term is the other loves its term in loving itself and loves itself in loving its term.* How much bitterness and sorrow would be lifted from the world were this simple law of being listened to and taken to heart? How much abnegation and self-sacrifice have withered into sterility because they came forth from hearts that hated themselves and wished to punish their own nothingness in a holocaust of good works? But there can be no true love of the other without a love of the self, and a true love of the other is simultaneously a love of the self. Man's ecstatic affirmation of the other is his affirmation of his own existence, an existence which is totally thrown out toward the world in an embrace as broad as being itself. This opening of man to being, together with this fulfilling of being by man, is the ecstasy in which history is born. It is an ecstasy defining the Catholic affirmation of being, and the Catholic order stands to this ecstasy of love in a relation which is proportionate to Protestantism's salute to the courage to be.

Professor Tillich declares, without any condescension on his part, that Catholic courage is "the courage to be a part," whereas Protestant courage is quite simply "the courage to be."[81] Seeking salvation within the Church, participating in the sacraments which are the common bread of the faithful, having his being in the One Mystical Body of whom he is a part in and through the Love who is the Spirit of God, the Catholic is not the silent figure of Dürer's knight riding through the desert. The Catholic tradition has always considered the faithful to form a company and for that reason the very meaning of the "I" is its fulfillment in a "we." If the Holy Trinity in the symbolic language of Tillich is a dialectical conquest over nothingness and finiteness, then the Spirit of God—in the ancient language of the *Fides Catholica*—is the Love between Father and Son forming with Them a subsisting "We," a Holy Company.[82] Chesterton once wrote in an awful illumination whose light lifts the darkness of hell "that it is not well for God to be alone."[83] The corporate and ecstatic structure of Catholic culture not only reflects the structure of being, but it is an analogue of the inner Life of the One Lord who is Himself a Society.

Catholic civilizations can be rich and somber; they can be militant, as were the youth of the Crusades; they can create the nervous genius and the grotesque of the cathedrals; they can give away their sons to the anonymity of leprosariums hidden under the decency of palms. It was a Catholic vision of reality that brought forth the splendor of the Baroque: the age of the cavalier and the duel, of the closed carriage and the silver cane, of churches as gay as the ballrooms they resembled. The Catholic vision can be fitted to the cloth of any people, but the culture that issues therefrom will always be ecstatic. Where the tragic sense of life is underdeveloped or sentimentalized, Catholic ecstasy is buoyant and playful, as in the peasant Baroque of Austria where even the cemeteries are a riot of bouncing cherubs and joyous angels. Where the tragic is intensified, as in Spain with her death-directed dynamism, the ecstasy called forth is all the more piercing and reaches to an affirmation of the Eternal that is born of a love that refuses to settle for anything less than Divinity. "Everything or nothing," says St. John of the Cross, and "in dying I live and in living I die," says St. Teresa of Avila. But whether or not the primacy of love be heightened by a sense of the finiteness and tragedy of existence as in Spain, the Catholic world never husbands its strength against the demonic within, but always expends its substance upon the world without.

Paul Tillich reminds us that the word *trotz*—"in spite of" —recurs constantly in the writings of Martin Luther. The Protestant of tomorrow will meet the new world in spite of the anxieties it brings, in spite of the heroism that it demands. He will confront the darkness of outer space with the courage he has inherited from his fathers of the Reformation. But we Catholics have an inheritance all our own— the inheritance of folly. All love is folly because all love is based on the impossible paradox that a man will gain his soul only by throwing it away. But the more we are dwarfed by the stars beyond, the more we shall love them as creatures of the Triune God. And the more we love them, the more will they be brought low and the more will we be exalted above them. We shall know all these things, but we shall not love because of this knowledge. And this love will be our Catholic courage—the courage of fools.

Notes

1. Paul Tillich, *The Courage to Be* (New Haven: Yale University Press, 1954), p. 190.
2. *Ibid.*, p. 188.

3. Paul Tillich, *Systematic Theology* (Chicago: University of Chicago Press, 1957), Vol. II, p. 12.

4. Chesterton, *Orthodoxy*, pp. 256–257.

5. Tillich, *op. cit.*, p. 12.

6. *Ibid.*, Vol, I, pp. 18–28.

7. Tillich, e.g., *ibid.*, Vol. II, pp. 48–49; *The Courage to Be*, pp. 86–135.

8. Tillich, *Systematic Theology*, Vol. II, pp. 48–49.

9. Christopher Dawson, *The Dynamics of World History* (London: Sheed & Ward, 1957), esp. the chapter, "Catholicism and the Bourgeois Mind"; cf. my own studies, "The Vision of Christopher Dawson," *The Commonweal*, Vol. LXVII, No. 14 (Jan. 3, 1958); "Jacques Maritain y el espiritu del barroco," *Nuestro Tiempo* (Pamplona), No. 58 (April 1959), pp. 383–403.

10. Tillich, *op. cit.*, Vol. II, p. 19.

11. *Ibid.*

12. *Ibid.*, Vol. I, p. 238.

13. *Ibid.*, pp. 25–26, 153–154.

14. *Ibid.*, Vol. II, pp. 21–22.

15. *Ibid.*, p. 20.

16. *Ibid.*

17. *Ibid.*, p. 21.

18. *Ibid.*, p. 23.

19. *Ibid.*, pp. 22–23.

20. Paul Tillich, *Love, Power, and Justice* (New York and London: Oxford University Press, 1954), p. 19.

21. *Ibid.*, *passim*.

22. *Ibid.*, p. 24.

23. Tillich, *Systematic Theology*, Vol. I, p. 113.

24. Jacques Maritain, *A Preface to Metaphysics* (New York: Sheed & Ward, 1940).

25. Tillich, *Systematic Theology*, Vol. I, p. 113.

26. *Ibid.*

27. May and others, *Existence*, p. 43.

28. Tillich, *op. cit.*, pp. 112–113.

29. *Ibid.*, p. 113.

30. *Ibid.*, p. 182; cf. also *The Courage to Be*, p. 34.

31. *Ibid.*, p. 187.

32. Tillich, *The Courage to Be*, pp. 88–89, 159–160, 172–173;

Love, Power, and Justice, pp. 35–54; *Systematic Theology*, Vol. I, pp. 230–231, 235–237, 272–273.

33. Tillich, *The Courage to Be*, pp. 22–26.

34. *Ibid.*, p. 179.

35. Tillich, *The Courage to Be*, p. 172; "You are Accepted," *The Shaking of the Foundations* (New York: Charles Scribner's Sons, 1948), pp. 153–164.

36. Tillich, *The Courage to Be*, p. 172.

37. *Ibid.*, pp. 58–59.

38. Thomas Mann, *Doctor Faustus* (cf. the remarkable dialogue between Dr. Faustus and the devil in the light of Tillich's observations on late medieval anxiety); Hilaire Belloc, *Paris*, esp. pp. 203–271.

39. The judgment is not that of Tillich but of Eric Ritter von Kuehnelt-Leddihn, *Freiheit oder Gleichheit* (Salzburg: Otto Müller Verlag, 1953), esp. pp. 323–362. The author maintains the thesis that Lutheranism was a reaction back to the late Middle Ages.

40. Tillich, *op. cit.*, p. 167.

41. *Ibid.*, p. 161.

42. Tillich, *Systematic Theology*, Vol. I, pp. 48–49.

43. Tillich, *Love, Power, and Justice*, pp. 47–50.

44. *Ibid.*, p. 33.

45. Tillich, *The Courage to Be*, p. 30.

46. Tillich, *Systematic Theology*, Vol. I, p. 229.

47. A lower case "t" is used for the trinitarian structure of the ground of being as accessible to ontology; the upper case is reserved for the specifically Christian mystery.

48. Tillich, *op. cit.*, p. 56; cf. pp. 53–59 for the whole argument summarized in the paragraph above.

49. *Ibid.*, p. 56.

50. *Ibid.*

51. Tillich, *The Courage to Be*, p. 180. Italics added.

52. Tillich, *Systematic Theology*, Vol. II, p. 144.

53. *Ibid.*, p. 143.

54. *Ibid.*, p. 143; also Vol. I, pp. 226–230.

55. *Ibid.*, Vol. I, p. 229.

56. *Ibid.*, p. 251. Italics added.

57. *Ibid.*, p. 251. (It is difficult to see how the ground of being could be *both* the sterility of the idea of absolute being divorced

from non-being *and* the demonic, if separated from the concept of the logos. The demonic implies the dynamic and the active in opposition to the passivity of the Hegelian "pure being." Tillich does not reconcile these two positions, at least so far as I can judge. Possibly Tillich means to say that the idea of pure being projected into reality would have to be demonic. In any event, his teaching on this point remains obscure.)

58. *Ibid.*

59. Zubiri, *Naturaleza, Historia, Dios,* "Los supuestos de una filosofiia," pp. 153–157.

60. Whittaker Chambers, "The Coming Struggle for Outer Space," *National Review,* Nov. 2, 1957, p. 399.

61. Frederick D. Wilhelmsen, Introduction to Romano Guardini, *The End of the Modern World* (London: Sheed & Ward, 1957), p. 6.

62. Zubiri, *op. cit.,* p. 155–156.

63. Plato, *Republic,* B. VI, 844 a.

64. Guardini, *The End of the Modern World,* p. 19.

65. Tillich, *The Courage to Be,* pp. 35–39, 45, 80.

66. Voegelin, *Order and History,* Vol. 1, *Israel and Revelation.* Cf. especially the introduction.

67. Voegelin, *Order and History,* Vol. 2, *The World of the Polis,* pp. 84–92.

68. *Ibid.*

69. Antonio Millan Puelles, *El logicismo platonico y la intuicion metafisica del ser* (Madrid: C. Bermejo, Impesor, 1958), p. 154.

70. Charles Cochrane, *Christianity and Classical Culture* (Oxford: Oxford University Press, 1957), Chap. XII, pp. 456–516.

71. Gerald Smith, S.J., *Natural Theology* (New York: Macmillan, 1958), p. 225.

72. D. B. J. Hawkins, *Being and Becoming* (London and New York: Sheed & Ward, 1954), p. 42.

73. Joseph Owens, "The Object of Metaphysics," *The New Scholasticism,* Vol. XXVIII (October 1954), p. 466–468.

74. Pedro Cabra, "La accion en la metafisica presencial," *Revista de Filosofía,* Vol. XVIII, No. 68 (1959), p. 58.

75. Aquinas, *De Ente et Essentia,* C. IV.

76. Cf. Owens, *op. cit., passim;* Domingo Bañez, *Schol. Com. in 1, 3, 4* (Salm. 1585), tomo I, col. 212/E-213/B. (This last is pos-

sibly the finest commentary on *esse*-essence within traditional Dominican Thomism.)

77. Owens, *op. cit., passim.*

78. *Ibid.,* p. 459–460. Cf. the article by the same author, Owens, "The Accidental and Essential Character of Being in the Doctrine of St. Thomas Aquinas," *Medieval Studies,* Vol. XX (1958).

79. Chesterton, *op. cit.* p. 132–133.

80. *Summa Theologiae,* II–II, Q. 64, a. 5, *corpus.*

81. Tillich, *The Courage to Be,* pp. 94–103.

82. We refer the reader once again to the remarkable study by Xavier Zubiri, *Naturaleza, Historia, Dios,* especially pp. 341–371.

83. Chesterton, *op. cit.,* p. 252.